Eyewitness
Train

Jigsaw puzzle featuring *Thomas the Tank Engine*

Midland Railway coat of arms

MIDLAND

Railway ticket

Model of 1843 Norris locomotive

AUSTRIA

Signal box bell tapper

Preserved 1938 steam locomotive *Duchess of Hamilton*

46229

Eyewitness
Train

Written by
JOHN COILEY

Metal whistle

Columbine steam
locomotive, 1845

French railways free pass

Railway police batons

DUCHESS OF HAMILTON

in association with
THE NATIONAL RAILWAY MUSEUM · YORK

Model of American
steam locomotive, 1875

Royal train
headlamp

Mechanical
semaphore signal

DK

LONDON, NEW YORK,
MELBOURNE, MUNICH, AND DELHI

Project editor Christine Webb
Art editor Ann Cannings
Managing editor Helen Parker
Managing art editor Julia Harris
Production Louise Barratt
Picture research Cynthia Hole
Special photography Mike Dunning

REVISED EDITION
Consultants Robert Gwynne and Russel Hollowood
of the National Rail Museum
Editors Jayne Miller, Steve Setford
Art editors Edward Kinsey, Peter Radcliffe
Managing editor Camilla Hallinan
Managing art editor Owen Peyton Jones
Art director Martin Wilson
Associate publisher Andrew Macintyre
Production editor Laragh Kedwell
Production controller Pip Tinsley
Picture research Myriam Megharbi

Passenger tickets

Late 19th-century
pocket watch

This Eyewitness ® Guide has been conceived by
Dorling Kindersley Limited and Editions Gallimard

First published in Great Britain in 1992
This revised edition published in 2009 by
Dorling Kindersley Limited, 80 Strand, London WC2R ORL

2 4 6 8 10 9 7 5 3 1
ED774 – 02/09

Carriage
keys

A CIP catalogue record for this book is available from the British Library

ISBN: 978-1-40533-782-3

Colour reproduction by Colourscan, Singapore
Printed by Toppan Co., (Shenzen) Ltd., China

Station
handbell

Discover more at
www.dk.com

Contents

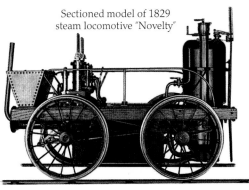

Sectioned model of 1829
steam locomotive "Novelty"

6
What is a train?
8
The first railways
10
Dawn of the steam age
12
Steam engines come of age
14
How a steam locomotive works
16
Railways reach the world
18
The American railroad
20
Building the railways
22
Overcoming obstacles
24
Making tracks
26
Freight trains
28
First, second, and third class
30
Travelling in style
32
In the signal box
34
Following the signs
36
Post haste
38
Electric trains
40
Diesel power

42
Long distance by train
44
Royal trains
46
Record breakers
48
At the station
50
Running the railway
52
Still in steam
54
All decked out
56
Travelling underground
58
Up in the air
60
Trains for fun
62
Into the future
64
Great train journeys
66
Train timeline
68
Find out more
70
Glossary
72
Index

What is a train?

A TRAIN IS A SERIES OF VEHICLES on wheels, and is either pulled by a locomotive or self-propelled. It is an integral part of a railway – a track that carries and guides trains along it. Railways of one form or another were used long before the first steam train came into existence. The earliest trains relied on human power to push or pull them along the tracks. Horses were even stronger than people, and could pull heavier loads. But it was the invention of the steam locomotive that led to the potential of a railway system being fully appreciated. Steam trains were far more powerful. With smoother, stronger tracks, they could run faster, hauling both people and goods. Starting with the first steam locomotive in the early 1800s, the railways advanced rapidly. With the help of modern engineering techniques, diesel and electric locomotives are still improving the quality of the railways today.

MUSCLE POWER
The earliest railways were built for private use, such as in mines. When longer public lines had to be constructed, armies of builders were needed, since very little specialised equipment was available. The builders, or "navvies", had to dig and shift soil, lay tracks, and build bridges and tunnels using hand tools and sheer muscle power.

DAY TRIPPERS
Steam trains had become a familiar sight by the end of the 19th century. They made it possible for people living in the country near big cities to commute into the city for work, or for pleasure. City-dwellers could also enjoy a trip to the country or the seaside.

A reproduction 1830 first-class carriage from the Liverpool and Manchester line

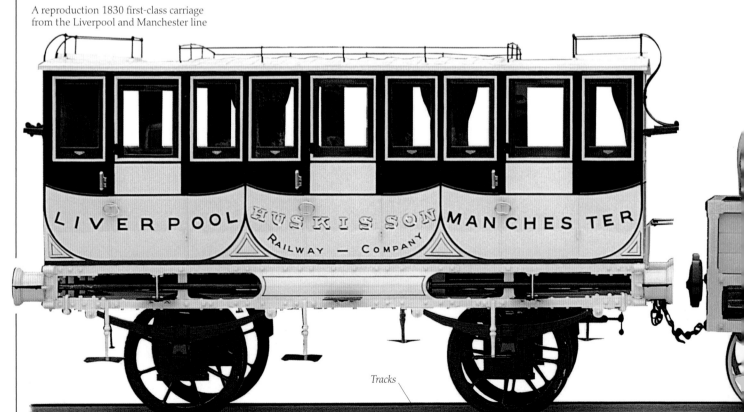

LIVERPOOL HUSKISSON MANCHESTER
RAILWAY — COMPANY

Tracks

DIESEL TRAINS

The first successful diesel trains were introduced in the 1930s on passenger services in Europe and the USA. Ten years later, diesel-electric locomotives were replacing even the largest steam locomotives. The days of steam were over. Today diesel power is used worldwide (pp. 40–41).

PASSENGER TRAINS

Nowadays, huge numbers of passengers travel on the railways every day. Passenger trains have developed significantly from the early days of the 1820s and 1830s, when many carriages were little more than open wagons with seats (pp. 28–29). Carriages were gradually equipped with lighting, heating, lavatories, and corridors. For longer journeys, sleeping and dining cars were provided.

ELECTRIC TRAINS

Electric trains first ran on an underground railway in the 1890s (pp. 56–57). They take their power from overhead cables, or from a live rail on the track. Electric trains are faster, quieter, and cleaner, without the pollution produced by diesel or steam locomotives. All new railways, whether between or within cities, are likely to be electric (pp. 38–39).

LOCOMOTIVE POWER

Trains carry passengers or freight – and sometimes both. They run on tracks, and have wheels with a lip, or flange, fitting inside the rails, so guiding the train. The first trains, like this modern reproduction, were hauled by steam locomotives. Nowadays, most trains are hauled by diesel or electric locomotives.

MOVING GOODS

The earliest trains were built to move freight, which was mainly coal (pp. 26–27). Today, railways remain an important method of moving freight, although traffic in most countries has declined dramatically due to competition from road transport.

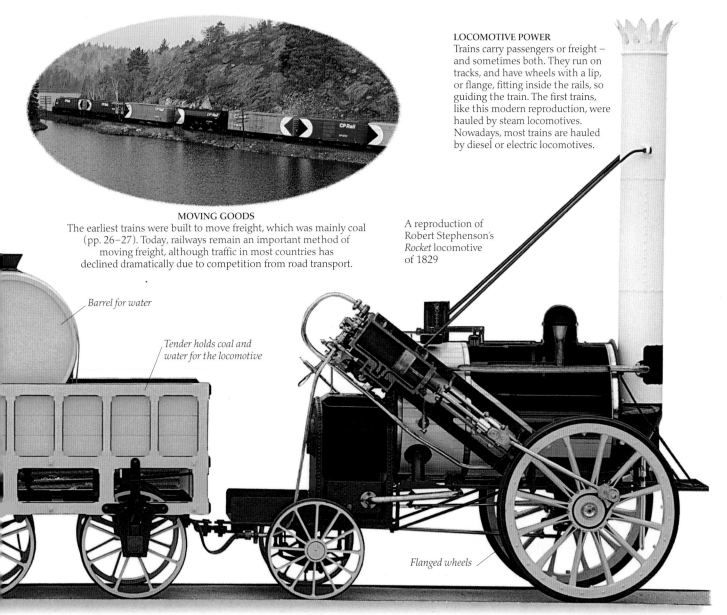

A reproduction of Robert Stephenson's *Rocket* locomotive of 1829

Barrel for water

Tender holds coal and water for the locomotive

Flanged wheels

The first railways

RAILWAYS EXISTED LONG BEFORE steam engines were invented. The railways that we know today have developed from the ones first used in European mines in the mid-16th century. To make manual work easier, heavy loads were transported in wagons with four wheels, running on parallel wooden planks. A peg fixed under the wagon slotted into the gap between the planks, guiding the wagon. Later railways had different guiding systems. Some had rails with flanges, or lips, to stop the wheels from slipping off. Others had smooth rails, and the wheels had a flange to keep them on the rails (pp. 24–25). Until the steam locomotive came along, the main means of hauling the loads was either human power or horsepower.

ANCIENT ROADWAYS
Evidence of tracks which guide vehicles travelling along them, the basic principle of a railway, can still be found in Mediterranean countries. Early civilizations, such as the Babylonians and the Sumerians, were aware of the benefits of roadways made out of stone slabs. Because these roadways had uneven surfaces, grooves were cut in the stone blocks to help guide the vehicles. Grooved stone tracks made by the Romans can still be seen in the ruins of Pompeii (above).

EASY RIDER
Some of the earliest railways in Britain were used to take coal from collieries to ships on the nearby rivers. In general, much of this journey was downhill and the brakes-man had to control the wagon's descent. To conserve their energy for the long uphill haul, pulling the empty wagons back to the colliery, many horses had a downhill ride in a special wagon, such as this one known as a dandy cart.

This dandy cart was used to transport a horse downhill

STAGECOACH
The stagecoach was the fastest means of transport before railways. Relays of horses for stagecoaches, and fast mail coaches travelling at an average speed of about 11.3 kph (7 mph) greatly reduced journey times.

HUMAN POWER
This engraving, published in 1752, was the first illustration of an English railway. The railway was apparently hand-operated. It is also the first recorded use of a flanged wheel on a railway in Britain.

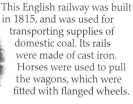

HEAVY LOADS

This English railway was built in 1815, and was used for transporting supplies of domestic coal. Its rails were made of cast iron. Horses were used to pull the wagons, which were fitted with flanged wheels.

JAPANESE HORSEPOWER

Horse-powered railways were widely used throughout the world to pull vehicles for passengers and freight until the early 1900s, and in some cases long afterwards.

DELIVERING COAL

Loaded coal wagons, or chaldrons, descended through gravity to their destination point. This brakes-man can be seen controlling the wagon's speed by sitting on the handle of a simple lever brake, while the horse follows behind.

EARLY GERMAN RAILWAYS

Although horses had been used to pull loads on wagon ways in Germany since the 18th century, the first steam railway in Germany did not open until 1835 (pp. 16–17).

A wagon-load of coal became a measure of coal known as a "chaldron"

COAL CARRIER

Chaldron was the name given to the wooden wagon used to carry coal from collieries in the northeast of England to the River Tyne, where it was further transported by sea. The chaldron was loaded from above at the colliery. When on the wooden wharf (platform) over the river, it discharged coal through a door in the floor, directly into a ship waiting below.

Brake lever

Flanged wheel

Dawn of the steam age

Ever since the first practical steam engines were designed by Thomas Newcomen in 1712, and James Watt in 1769, engineers tried to use this steam power to drive a self-propelled vehicle. The first vehicle of this kind was difficult to control and caused such an uproar in the streets of Paris that the project was abandoned. It was not until the early 19th century that the first successful guided railway locomotives were designed, although there were still many technical problems to overcome. The engines had to be powerful enough to pull a heavy load, and make as little noise and smoke as possible. They also had to run on smooth rails that would not break under their weight, and which the wheels could grip without slipping.

LOCAL ATTRACTION
This engraving shows a locomotive built in 1808 by Richard Trevithick. It pulled a four-wheeled carriage round a circular track, and was open to the public. This was the first steam locomotive to run in London. Because of the circular track, the locomotive became known as *Catch-me-who-can*.

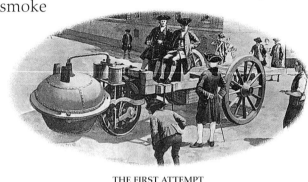

THE FIRST ATTEMPT
In 1769, Frenchman Nicholas Cugnot built the first self-propelled vehicle in the world. His three-wheeled steam-powered road vehicle reached a speed of 14.5 kph (9 mph). However, it was difficult to control in a street full of people and horse-drawn carriages. The resulting uproar led Cugnot to abandon the project.

CATCH ME WHO CAN
This model is based on drawings of the locomotive built by Richard Trevithick in 1808. Trevithick was the engineer of the world's first working steam locomotive, built in 1804. It hauled a train of coal-wagons and 70 men.

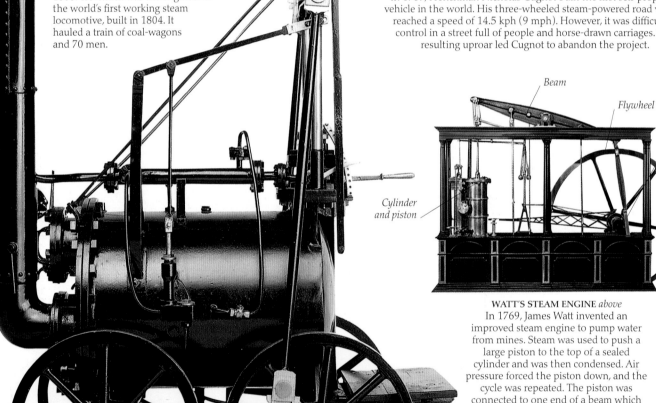

Beam

Flywheel

Crank

Cylinder and piston

WATT'S STEAM ENGINE *above*
In 1769, James Watt invented an improved steam engine to pump water from mines. Steam was used to push a large piston to the top of a sealed cylinder and was then condensed. Air pressure forced the piston down, and the cycle was repeated. The piston was connected to one end of a beam which rocked back and forth. The other end of the beam turned a flywheel via a crank. This power was used to operate the water pumps. Such an engine was, however, far too heavy and cumbersome for a locomotive.

Flanged rails to guide smooth wheels

BY LAND AND BY WATER

The first self-propelled land vehicle in America was this scow (a type of boat), built by the blacksmith and boatbuilder Oliver Evans in 1804. It ran on wheels under its own steam. When it reached water, the wheels were removed and it continued its journey by water.

GETTING A GRIP

In their search for the perfect locomotive, early engineers tried to improve the grip of the wheels on the rails. In this 1812 engraving the locomotive's driving wheel fits onto a toothed rack running alongside the smooth rails, giving extra grip.

CHAOS

This 1828 cartoon is an artist's impression of what the streets of London might have looked like with the coming of steam-powered road vehicles.

PUFFING BILLY

Puffing Billy was built by William Hedley in Wylam, northern England, in 1813. It was used to haul coal wagons from a colliery to a nearby river, a distance of about 8 km (5 miles). It proved that, with the right design, there was sufficient grip between a smooth driving wheel and a smooth rail for a locomotive to pull a commercial load. Because of complaints about the noise and smoke that it made, *Puffing Billy* was modified so that the steam passed through a "quieting" chamber before going up the chimney.

Puffing Billy is one of the two oldest surviving steam locomotives in the world

Coal shovel used on *Puffing Billy*

The driver stood here

Fuel supply

Steam locomotives come of age

Polish stamp showing a locomotive built by Robert Stephenson

IT WAS THE VISION OF Englishman George Stephenson, the "father of railways", that led the way to the age of steam. Stephenson saw that the steam locomotive was the way forward for the railways. Together with his son Robert, he established his locomotive works in 1823, and began to build steam locomotives for Britain and around the world. By the mid-19th century, the steam locomotive had been adopted worldwide by virtue of its strength, simplicity, and reliability. The basic principles of the steam locomotive's design were to remain essentially unchanged until diesel-electric and electric locomotives signalled the end of the age of steam (pp. 38–41).

STEAM FOR THE PEOPLE
The Stockton and Darlington Railway opened in England in 1825, and was the world's first public railway to use steam from the beginning. To start with, the locomotives on this line were reserved for goods trains. It was not until 1833 that they were used for passenger trains.

BEST FRIEND OF CHARLESTON
The *Best Friend of Charleston* was the first successful steam locomotive to be built in the USA. The *Best Friend* entered service in 1830, and operated the first regular steam service in the USA.

LIVERPOOL & MANCHESTER
Directors Ticket
RAILWAY.

Railway directors were provided with free passes for life

Engraved ivory free pass c. 1830

GLASGOW & SOUTH WESTERN

Gold and enamel free pass c. 1850

NOVELTY
In 1829, the Rainhill trials were held to choose a locomotive design for the new Liverpool and Manchester railway in England. Huge crowds gathered to see the entrants. One of them was *Novelty*. It was a very fast engine, but broke down too frequently.

Sectioned model of "Novelty"

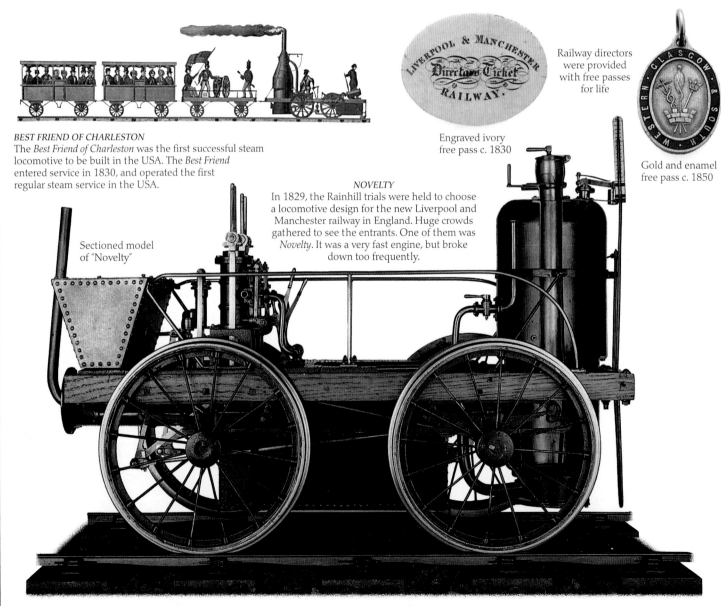

STEAM REACHES EUROPE
After the success of the Liverpool and Manchester Railway, steam railways were soon adopted all over Europe. This print shows a scene on the first railroad between Leipzig and Dresden in Germany in 1837.

AMERICAN CLASSICS
The steam passenger train was established in the USA by the mid-19th century. American locomotives could not be mistaken – they had large headlamps, wooden "cowcatchers" for sweeping animals off the line, and bronze warning bells.

Robert Stephenson

FLYING SCOTSMAN
By the 1920s, famous express trains ran throughout the world. One of the most famous was the *Flying Scotsman*, which travelled 633 km (392.7 miles) between London and Edinburgh, in Scotland.

WINNER TAKES ALL
Rocket is one of the most famous locomotives in the world. It entered the 1829 Rainhill trials, and won the competition. In doing so it established, once and for all, the superiority of the steam locomotive over the horse as a means of power for railways. It was Robert Stephenson who was largely responsible for the design of *Rocket*.

Rocket locomotive, built in 1829

How a steam locomotive works

THE DESIGN OF ALL STEAM LOCOMOTIVES is based on the same principles which governed the building of the very first ones. First, a coal fire in the firebox heats up water in the boiler, producing steam. This steam is used to move a piston back and forth. The movement of the piston turns the wheels via a connecting rod and crank. In all, it takes about three hours for the hardworking crew to make a locomotive get up enough steam to move.

American steam
locomotive

WHEEL ARRANGEMENTS
Different classes of steam locomotive are often described by their wheel arrangements. For example, this locomotive has a 4–6–2 wheel arrangement, composed of four leading wheels, six driving wheels, and two trailing wheels.

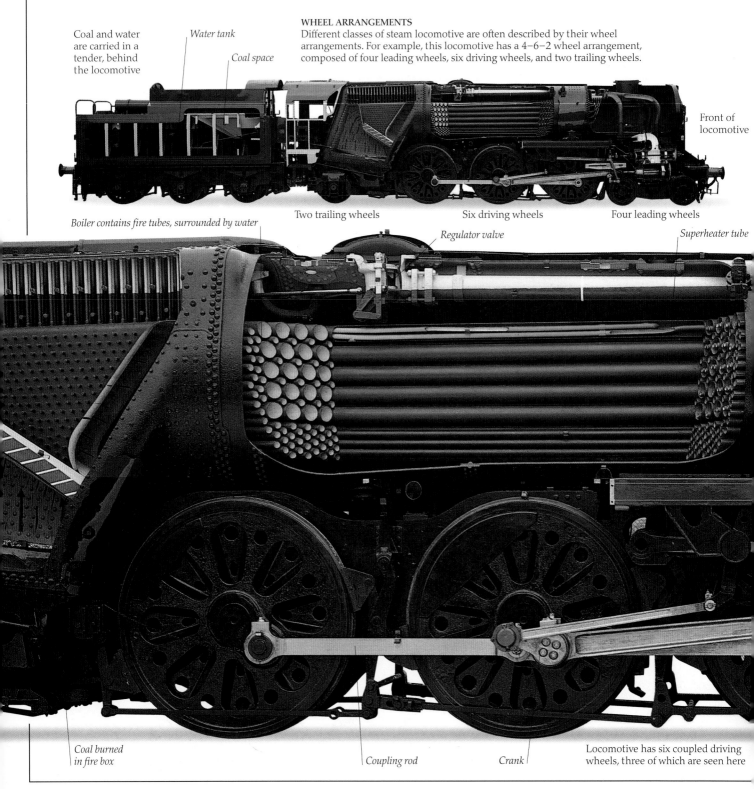

Coal and water are carried in a tender, behind the locomotive

Water tank

Coal space

Front of locomotive

Boiler contains fire tubes, surrounded by water

Two trailing wheels

Six driving wheels

Four leading wheels

Regulator valve

Superheater tube

Coal burned in fire box

Coupling rod

Crank

Locomotive has six coupled driving wheels, three of which are seen here

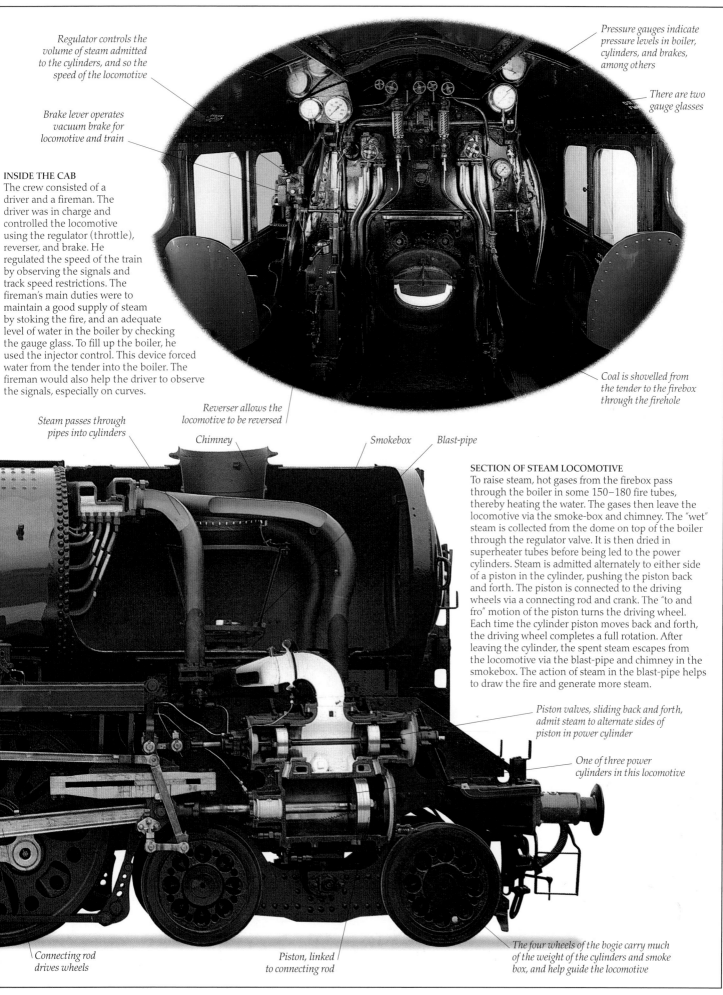

Regulator controls the volume of steam admitted to the cylinders, and so the speed of the locomotive

Brake lever operates vacuum brake for locomotive and train

Pressure gauges indicate pressure levels in boiler, cylinders, and brakes, among others

There are two gauge glasses

INSIDE THE CAB
The crew consisted of a driver and a fireman. The driver was in charge and controlled the locomotive using the regulator (throttle), reverser, and brake. He regulated the speed of the train by observing the signals and track speed restrictions. The fireman's main duties were to maintain a good supply of steam by stoking the fire, and an adequate level of water in the boiler by checking the gauge glass. To fill up the boiler, he used the injector control. This device forced water from the tender into the boiler. The fireman would also help the driver to observe the signals, especially on curves.

Coal is shovelled from the tender to the firebox through the firehole

Reverser allows the locomotive to be reversed

Steam passes through pipes into cylinders

Chimney

Smokebox

Blast-pipe

SECTION OF STEAM LOCOMOTIVE
To raise steam, hot gases from the firebox pass through the boiler in some 150–180 fire tubes, thereby heating the water. The gases then leave the locomotive via the smoke-box and chimney. The "wet" steam is collected from the dome on top of the boiler through the regulator valve. It is then dried in superheater tubes before being led to the power cylinders. Steam is admitted alternately to either side of a piston in the cylinder, pushing the piston back and forth. The piston is connected to the driving wheels via a connecting rod and crank. The "to and fro" motion of the piston turns the driving wheel. Each time the cylinder piston moves back and forth, the driving wheel completes a full rotation. After leaving the cylinder, the spent steam escapes from the locomotive via the blast-pipe and chimney in the smokebox. The action of steam in the blast-pipe helps to draw the fire and generate more steam.

Piston valves, sliding back and forth, admit steam to alternate sides of piston in power cylinder

One of three power cylinders in this locomotive

Connecting rod drives wheels

Piston, linked to connecting rod

The four wheels of the bogie carry much of the weight of the cylinders and smoke box, and help guide the locomotive

Railways reach the world

THE OPENING OF THE FIRST "modern" railway in England, in 1830, aroused interest from all over the world. People from many countries came to see and travel on it. When these countries set up their own railways, many chose to follow British designs for locomotives, carriages, and track. At first, equipment was made in Britain. Each country started to modify the designs and soon began to build its own equipment. By the mid-1830s, the USA was exporting steam locomotives to Europe. The railways had a great impact on all aspects of life in many countries, from trade to travel. In the USA, for example, they spanned the vast distances that had been a barrier to opening up the continent.

GERMANY'S FIRST
The first steam-operated railway in Germany was opened in 1835 between Nuremberg and Fürth on a line 8 km (5 miles) long. The English-built locomotive, seen here, was called *Der Adler*.

INDIAN LOCOMOTIVE
The strong British influence in India until 1947 meant that much railway equipment, including locomotives and carriages, was supplied from Britain. This model shows a typical design of steam locomotive built in Britain for use on the East Indian Railways. Details, such as the sun blinds on the cab windows and the large headlamp, were specially added.

ORIENTAL RAILWAYS
The first steam-worked railway line in Japan opened in 1872. This 19th-century woodblock contrasts modern transport technology of the time – the steam locomotive – with Japan's traditional forms of transport, such as horse-drawn and human-drawn carriages.

Hand rail

Power unit

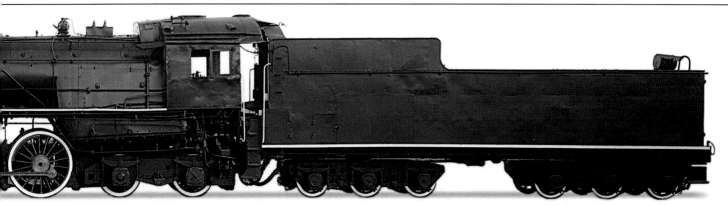

PARISIAN STEAM
The opening of public railways aroused much interest. This painting shows the first public steam railway in France which opened in 1837. The line ran northwest from Paris to Le Pecq.

CUSTOM-BUILT
This powerful locomotive was designed and built in Britain in the mid-1930s, for use on the Chinese National Railway. The locomotive is wider and higher than would be possible for use in Britain or Europe. The tender is very large, as it is necessary to carry as much water and coal as possible to work heavy trains over long distances.

MADE IN THE USA
This locomotive model is of a design by William Norris of Philadelphia, built in 1843 and exported to Austria. It was specially designed to work on lines with steep inclines and sharp curves.

Much more powerful articulated (jointed) locomotives of this type (known as a Beyer-Garratt), were later used in countries in Africa, as well as in India, Australia, and Britain

TRAVELLING HOME
This locomotive was built in Britain in 1909 to use in Tasmania. It is now operational on the Welsh Highland Railway, painted black. It was the first Garratt train, a new type of articulated locomotive, made of joined sections, designed for use on lines with sharp curves. Powerful locomotives of this type were made up of two steam power units.

The American railroad

THE GOLDEN SPIKE
On 10 May 1869, the USA was finally crossed by a railroad from east to west when the last spike, made of gold, was driven to join the Union Pacific Railroad to the Central Pacific Railroad.

FEW NATIONS have had their history and development so greatly influenced by a new mode of transport as the USA. In Europe the new railways were made to serve existing cities, but in the USA the railways themselves created many of the centres of population in what had been a huge, relatively empty continent. Progress was very rapid. By 1869, people could cross the continent, from east to west, by rail. In the early 20th century, most North Americans lived within 40 km (25 miles) of a railway. Since then, the fortunes of the railroads have declined, largely as a result of competition from road and air transport. Today, there are signs of a rail revival in areas where the advantages of the electric railway, in avoiding city road congestion and pollution, have been recognized.

A tall chimney improved the draught on the fire and made the locomotive more efficient – but there could be no low bridges on the line!

TOM THUMB
In 1830 *Tom Thumb*, a small experimental locomotive, made its first run on the 21 km (13 mile) completed section of the Baltimore and Ohio Railroad. *Tom Thumb* also entered into a celebrated race, seen here, with a horse-drawn train. The horse won.

IT'S A FIRST
The *Stourbridge Lion*, the first steam locomotive with flanged wheels to run on rails in the USA, was built in England in 1829. It was very similar to *Agenoria* (above), which was built for use in England.

Wheel has lip, or flange

Driver's cab

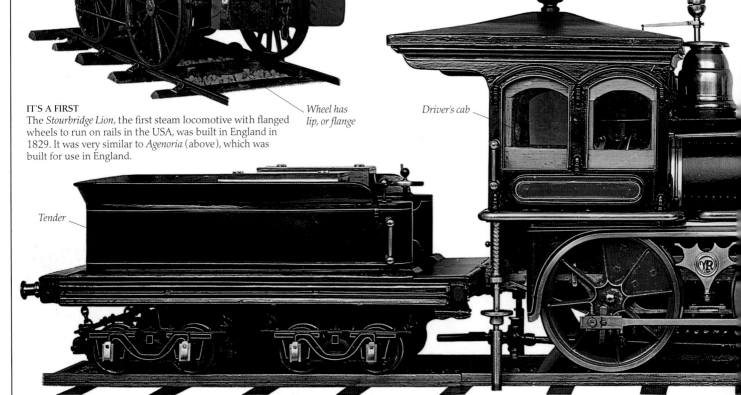

Tender

DE WITT CLINTON
The first steam train in New York State was hauled by the locomotive *De Witt Clinton* on 9 August 1831. The carriages were little more than stagecoaches. Passengers still rode on top of the vehicles, as well as inside.

BUILDING THE FUTURE
The opening up of the continent by the spread of railways was recognized as a great achievement with tremendous potential. The railways were to play an important part in the growth, and wealth, of many towns across the USA.

TROUBLESOME TIMES
During the construction of lines westwards from Chicago, trains were sometimes attacked by North American Indians. These were not unprovoked attacks – the locals were trying to defend their way of life, which was being threatened. The developers who appeared with the spread of the railroads were taking their land and hunting grounds from them.

Pivoted, or moving, axle

Cowcatcher keeps animals from derailing the locomotive

JOHN BULL
This was an early four-wheeled locomotive, designed by Robert Stephenson. It was shipped in sections from England in 1831. It soon displayed a tendency to derail, and became the first locomotive to be fitted with a two-wheeled pivoted axle in front of the driving wheels, together with a "cowcatcher" – a wedge shape at the front to deflect obstacles on the rail.

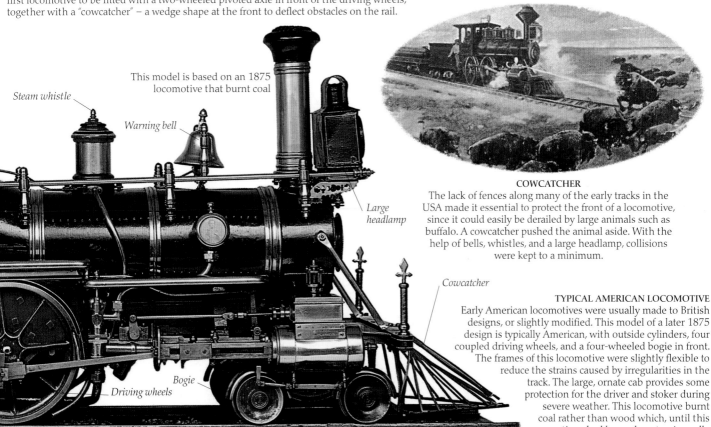

Steam whistle

Warning bell

This model is based on an 1875 locomotive that burnt coal

Large headlamp

Cowcatcher

Bogie

Driving wheels

COWCATCHER
The lack of fences along many of the early tracks in the USA made it essential to protect the front of a locomotive, since it could easily be derailed by large animals such as buffalo. A cowcatcher pushed the animal aside. With the help of bells, whistles, and a large headlamp, collisions were kept to a minimum.

TYPICAL AMERICAN LOCOMOTIVE
Early American locomotives were usually made to British designs, or slightly modified. This model of a later 1875 design is typically American, with outside cylinders, four coupled driving wheels, and a four-wheeled bogie in front. The frames of this locomotive were slightly flexible to reduce the strains caused by irregularities in the track. The large, ornate cab provides some protection for the driver and stoker during severe weather. This locomotive burnt coal rather than wood which, until this time, had been almost universally used in the USA.

Building the railways

Workman's pick

FAR MORE WORK goes into building a railway than might be expected. As trains cannot climb very steep hills, the shortest distance between two places may not be the easiest. Trains often have to follow longer, less hilly routes. To keep the railway route as level as possible, embankments, cuttings, bridges, and tunnels have to be built. The engineer in charge selects the route by deciding what the steepest slope, or gradient, can be. The type of trains which will use the railway, and the balance between speed and load, have to be taken into account. Very steep gradients can be avoided by spreading the route with "S"-shaped bends or spirals. To avoid making the route too long, tunnels and bridges may be built. These are expensive to build, but provide a much shorter and more level route.

HARD GRAFT
The most basic tools, such as this pick, were used to build early railways. Other equipment included shovels, shoulder hods (for carrying bricks), barrows, simple hoists, and wooden scaffolding. Gunpowder was used to blast the way through solid rock. The large number of workmen, or "navvies", who used the tools lived in makeshift temporary accommodation near the site.

BLOOD, SWEAT, AND TEARS
Early cuttings through rock, such as this 1831 example of a major cutting, were excavated with only primitive hand tools. A large workforce was needed, and the work took many years to complete. Much of the rock recovered was used to make stone sleepers on other railways.

THE CONSTRUCTION CREW
In the 19th century, American railways were usually built by crews living on site, in carriages attached to steam locomotives. The train would move the crews along the line as it was completed, as well as providing steam heating and hot water. Supplies and new rails were brought to the end of the line by other trains. Earth and rocks removed from cuttings were often used to build embankments. The wooden trestle bridge shown in the picture would have been built using local supplies.

American construction crew, 1885

BUILDING BRIDGES
When planning to build a bridge over a river, a temporary island of rocks must be made in the middle, or posts driven into the river bed. After this is done construction of the bridge can now begin. The parts of the bridge are floated down the river into position. This early wooden arch bridge was built on wooden piers, or trestles. The arch is shaped so that it counterbalances the point where the bridge will bend most under a heavy load. This design of bridge has been used extensively by the railways.

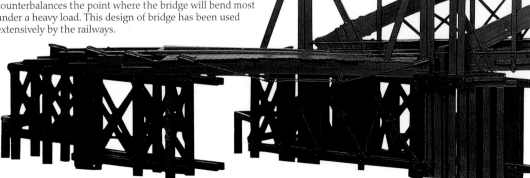

Model of 1848 wooden arch bridge

BRIDGES FOR TRAINS

There are many kinds of railway bridge – each with a specific design, depending on the local geography. Cantilever bridges are used when a large span, for example over water, is needed. Beam bridges arose from the simple concept of a tree trunk across a stream. These bridges usually have several supporting solid masonry piers, or sections. Trestle bridges, made from timber or steel, are similar to beam bridges. Arch bridges have a curved support on which the section carrying the track rests. Some bridges, such as the Royal Albert Bridge near Plymouth, England (left), are not based on one, but on a mixture of bridge designs.

Royal Albert Bridge, near Plymouth, designed by Isambard Kingdom Brunel in 1859

BRUNEL
Isambard Kingdom Brunel (1806–1859) was an outstanding mechanical and civil engineer. He was responsible for designing many of the great railways, bridges, and tunnels in Britain.

CHANNEL TUNNEL

Building a tunnel under the sea is a major feat of modern engineering. The Channel Tunnel provided the first ever rail link between Britain and France in 1994 (pp. 62–63). The tunnel is 49.8 km (31 miles) long, and is 38.6 km (24 miles) under the Channel and took six years to build. Construction work for underwater tunnels is highly automated. Tunnel-boring machines the diameter of the tunnel worked towards one another from both sides of the Channel. After the tunnels joined, the machines were buried since it was too difficult to remove them.

WHO PAYS?

Many railways have been financed by government-issued shares and bonds. Governments support the railways, as they are of both commercial and military importance. This gold bond certificate was issued by the U.S. government to finance railway construction. In many countries the railways have been taken over by the state, or maintained with a large government subsidy.

COMING AND GOING
Passenger stations (pp. 48–49) are designed to help the arrival and departure of passengers and to provide services while they are using the station.

Bridges on major rivers had to be high enough so that ships could pass underneath

Overcoming obstacles

As RAILWAY SYSTEMS GREW, increasing attention was given to the obstacles which limited or prevented their development. At first these were mainly physical, relating to the nature of land along the proposed route – such as deep valleys, hills and mountains, and wide rivers or lakes. Gradually, as engineering skills and techniques improved, these obstacles were overcome. Longer bridges were built in remote and difficult locations over deep valleys and gorges. Railways were developed that could climb up steep mountains. Today, the position is very different. There are many powerful, high-speed trains on purpose-built lines which are almost independent of the terrain they travel over. Nowadays, obstacles to railway operations and development are mostly economic and financial.

SYDNEY HARBOUR BRIDGE
The Sydney Harbour Bridge is probably best known for its characteristic shape on the Sydney skyline. But it is also famous for having the longest steel-arch span in the world – 503 m (1650 ft). When it opened in 1932, it carried two railway lines and two tram lines. Now it carries trains, eight road lanes, a footpath, and a cycle track.

STAYING POWER
Powerful locomotives were required for working trains in rugged country with steep gradients and tight curves. Normal locomotives of this type were usually long and heavy, which made it very difficult for them to go round the curves. One way around the problem was to adapt the wheels under the locomotive. Swivelling trolleys with wheels (bogies) were attached underneath the frame carrying the boiler. This enabled the locomotive to negotiate the tight curves.

Model of Kitson-Meyer type of tank locomotive built in 1903 for use in Chile

SAIL BY TRAIN
Train ferries came into use in the middle of the 19th century. Train Ferry 3 (pictured) ran on the Harwich-Zeebrugge route from 1924 to 1945 and carried freight.

RIGI RAILWAY
In 1873 a steam-operated railway was opened to the top of Mt. Rigi near Lucerne, using a rack and pinion system to climb steep gradients. It was the first such railway in Europe. A toothed rack was laid between the rails, and a powered cog on the locomotive drove the train up the mountain. Working in reverse, it helped to control the train's descent.

TOURIST ATTRACTION
Mountain climbing and sightseeing by steam railway became a great tourist attraction in the 19th century. The Snowdon Mountain Railway opened in Wales in 1896, and used a rack and pinion system (left) to climb the steep gradients.

CROSSING WATER
One of the greatest railway bridges ever constructed, the bridge over the Firth of Forth in Scotland, was opened in 1890. It is the oldest railway cantilever bridge (pp. 20–21) in the world, and is still in use today.

Although this locomotive had one boiler, it had two power units (each with a chimney), on swivelling bogies. These made it powerful enough for steep uphill stretches

C . N . R

MOUNT WASHINGTON COG RAILWAY
The world's first mountain rack railway opened in 1869 in New Hampshire, USA. This line originally used a wrought-iron rack, somewhat like a ladder, and had a maximum gradient of about 1 in 3 (one unit up for every three units along the slope). For a normal railway, a gradient of 1 in 30 is considered steep.

Swivelling power bogie for going around tight bends

Making tracks

RAILWAY LINES have been of fundamental importance to the history of trains. Rails were used to guide loaded wagons long before the steam locomotive came along. However, the early cast-iron rails were easily broken. It was not until stronger rails were available that the full potential of the steam locomotive could be exploited. Cast-iron rails were replaced by stronger, rolled wrought-iron rails, and since the 1870s, by steel which scarcely wears down. Tracks are constantly being improved to meet the requirements of heavier, faster trains. For a smoother ride, most main lines also have continuously welded rails, instead of the jointed short lengths which gave rise to the once familiar "clickety-click" sound of a train journey. The distance between the rails is known as the gauge and varies around the world. Many railways, especially those with difficult terrain to cross, have narrow gauge lines which are cheaper and faster to lay and maintain.

LAYING TRACKS
Building early railways was hard work and required large gangs of men working together to lift and position rails. Little equipment was available, but very often there was plentiful cheap labour. Today such work is almost entirely automated.

TRACK MARKS
The track layout at the approach to busy stations can be extremely complex. To enable trains to switch lines, special points (where trains change direction) were often provided, together with complicated diamond-patterned cross-overs on the track. Nowadays, such track layouts have been simplified, where possible.

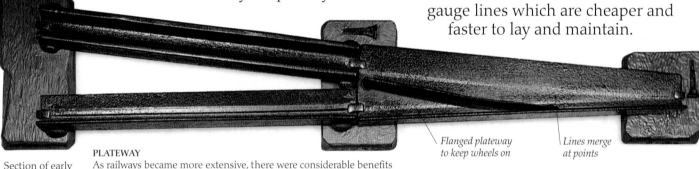

Flanged plateway to keep wheels on

Lines merge at points

Section of early plateway, 1799

PLATEWAY
As railways became more extensive, there were considerable benefits in being able to move a wagon from one line to another. This was done by merging two lines at points, or switches. Plateways (above), with their raised flanges, were not easily merged. They were replaced in the 1820s by smooth edge rails, for wagons with flanged wheels (with a lip on them), which made switches easier to construct.

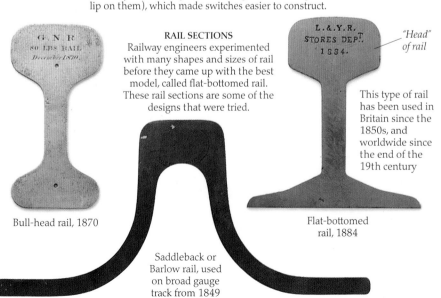

G N R
80 LBS RAIL
December 1870

RAIL SECTIONS
Railway engineers experimented with many shapes and sizes of rail before they came up with the best model, called flat-bottomed rail. These rail sections are some of the designs that were tried.

L.&.Y.R.
STORES DEPT.
1884.

"Head" of rail

This type of rail has been used in Britain since the 1850s, and worldwide since the end of the 19th century

Bull-head rail, 1870

Saddleback or Barlow rail, used on broad gauge track from 1849

Flat-bottomed rail, 1884

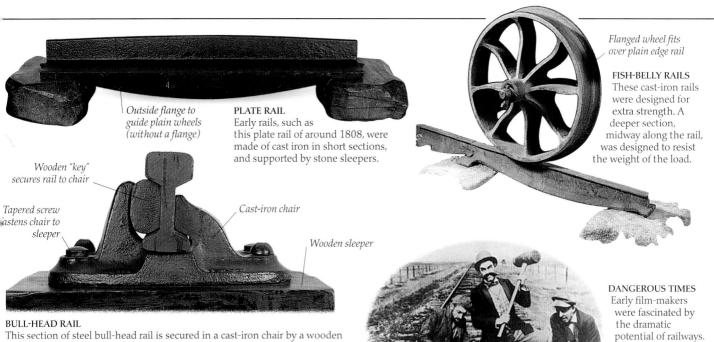

Outside flange to guide plain wheels (without a flange)

PLATE RAIL
Early rails, such as this plate rail of around 1808, were made of cast iron in short sections, and supported by stone sleepers.

Flanged wheel fits over plain edge rail

FISH-BELLY RAILS
These cast-iron rails were designed for extra strength. A deeper section, midway along the rail, was designed to resist the weight of the load.

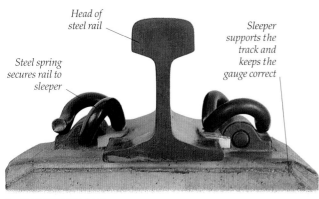

Wooden "key" secures rail to chair

Tapered screw fastens chair to sleeper

Cast-iron chair

Wooden sleeper

BULL-HEAD RAIL
This section of steel bull-head rail is secured in a cast-iron chair by a wooden "key". The chair is secured to a wooden sleeper by large screws.

Head of steel rail

Steel spring secures rail to sleeper

Sleeper supports the track and keeps the gauge correct

DANGEROUS TIMES
Early film-makers were fascinated by the dramatic potential of railways. Here the heroine is being tied to a track consisting of flat-bottomed rails.

FLAT-BOTTOMED RAIL
Modern flat-bottomed rails are made of steel. The rails are secured on a rubber pad, which is fastened to a concrete sleeper by means of a steel spring assembly. Early flat-bottomed rails would have been fastened directly by a spike to wooden sleepers.

MAKING CHANGES
Where railways with different gauges met, difficulties could arise. Changing trains was a considerable nuisance and effort for passengers, especially those with much luggage. The added costs of transferring freight from one train to another could also be very high.

GAUGE MEASURE
Special steel rails were used to check the gauge or distance between rails. The distance was measured from the inside edge of one rail to the inside edge of the other. The standard gauge in Britain, and in many other countries including most of Europe and North America, is 1,435 mm (4 ft 8.5 in). The broad gauge measure is wider, and the narrow gauge measure is less, than the standard gauge. However, the actual measurements for each of these gauges varies from country to country.

F.D.BANISTER Esq, C.E.

Freight trains

THE EARLIEST TRAINS were freight trains that carried loads of coal or mineral ores. At first these trains were limited to two or three simple wagons hauled by a horse. However, with the development of the steam locomotive (pp. 10–11) much longer trains could be operated, and at higher speeds, making rail freight more efficient and economical. As the railway network developed, similar trains were used to move raw materials to factories and to distribute the finished products. In the early days, all freight trains were very slow because their primitive brake systems could not stop the train fast enough in case of an emergency. Technical developments since then now mean that freight trains can run at speeds of over 100 kph (62 mph).

GO BY RAIL
Bulky loads have been carried on trains since the 1820s. This East German stamp shows how moving heavy goods by rail helps reduce road congestion.

PASSENGERS AND FREIGHT
The first public railways in the 1830s operated steam-hauled trains for both passengers and freight. A wide variety of freight was carried, including live animals until quite recently.

LMS
295987   20T

BRAKE VAN
Most freight trains used to run with wagons that were not connnected to brakes. The only means of controlling the train was to apply the brake on the locomotive, and the guard's hand brake on the "brake" van. Such brakes were so feeble that in order to control their speed even short trains had to travel no faster than 50 kph (30 mph).

SHEDDING THE LOAD
Modern freight trains carry goods in huge containers all made to a standard size (pp. 62–63). These can be stacked on top of each other and moved from train to ship, truck, or aircraft without unpacking. Before this, cranes had to unload masses of multi-sized containers from "wagon-load" trains to transfer freight to and from trucks.

DIESEL POWER
In 1939 in the USA, the diesel-electric locomotive proved that it could outclass steam. By the mid-1950s most freight trains were hauled by diesel engines.

UNITE

MI

Load not to exceed   Tons   Tare

Shunter's pole with metal hook

SAFETY FIRST
For many years wagons were joined by three chain links. It was the shunter's job to couple (join) and uncouple the wagons. When doing the job by hand, they risked being injured between the wagons, but they could do it quickly and safely by using a shunter's pole.

Coal wagon from the Stanton coal mine in the north of England

Side door for unloading

STANTON

9988

TARE 7~4~3

LOAD 12 TONS

Hand brake

COAL WAGON
Much of the freight traffic in Britain was made up of coal trains. For many years the coal was carried in simple wagons owned by individual coal mines, and had a capacity of around 10 tonnes (9 tons). The wagons were usually automatically loaded from above, but they often had to be unloaded by workers with shovels.

BULK LOADS
Most freight trains now haul bulky loads such as coal, oil, or building materials in purpose-built wagons. All wagons are fitted with air brakes operated by the driver. This means that they can safely run at more than 100 kph (60 mph).

TAIL-LIGHT
All trains carry a red tail lamp to indicate that they are complete. This modern electric battery version gives a flashing signal.

LINED DAIRIES TANK

44057

SHUNT WITH CARE

MILK TANKER
The coming of the railways helped to improve the public's diet and health by speedy delivery of milk and fish from rural areas to the cities. By the 1930s milk was transported in special glass-lined tankers that were fitted with driver-operated brakes.

First, second, and third class

THE FIRST PUBLIC passenger trains were a far cry from today's comfortable, spacious trains. They offered three different classes of accommodation, with those travelling in the greatest comfort paying the highest fare. The best, or first-class, accommodation was an enclosed compartment that looked very similar to a stagecoach. It had glass windows and padded seats. Second-class accommodation was an open wagon with seats, while the people in the third class had no seats. Travellers were not protected from rain or cold. As passenger trains were improved over the years, carriages were heated and corridors added, giving access to lavatories and to restaurant cars, as well as making ticket inspection an easier task.

PRIVATE ROOMS
First-class passengers travelled in spacious, comfortable carriages, and they were even able to hold private conversations. Travelling by rail in the second half of the 19th century was regarded as an enjoyable adventure in itself.

American first-class ticket

Australian second-class ticket

British third-class ticket

PAYING THE WAY
Tickets show that passengers have paid for their journey. These tickets look very much like the first card tickets that were made in 1837.

TICKET CLIPPERS
To indicate that a ticket has been used and inspected, it is clipped, marked, or stamped in some way.

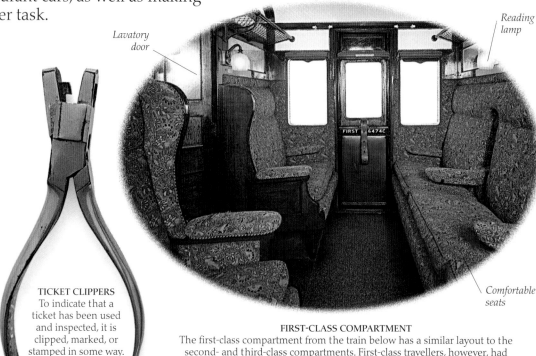

Lavatory door

Reading lamp

Comfortable seats

FIRST-CLASS COMPARTMENT
The first-class compartment from the train below has a similar layout to the second- and third-class compartments. First-class travellers, however, had more legroom and more comfortable and spacious seats. Passengers in this compartment had the smoothest journey, as they were farthest from the bumps and jolts of the wheels.

Third-class compartment

Lavatory

EARLY DAYS
The earliest images of steam passenger trains from the 1830s show the enclosed first-class carriages carrying luggage – and guards – on the roof. Second- and third-class vehicles were not enclosed.

Lavatory

A FRESH START
The development of railways and steamships during the 19th century opened the doors to large-scale immigration. This was particularly true in North America once railways linked the East Coast to the Middle West, and eventually the West Coast. When they had crossed the Atlantic, immigrants from all over Europe travelled westwards on very crowded trains.

SECOND-CLASS COMPARTMENT
Compared with first class, this compartment was simpler and had less legroom. Partly because there was very little difference between the second and either the first or third class, the second class almost completely disappeared from trains in Britain soon after this carriage was built.

Posters advertising railway destinations

HARD TIMES
In the early days, third-class travel was a far cry from first-class. Three or four times as many passengers of all ages were crowded into the same space.

THIRD-CLASS COMPARTMENT
This compartment had the simplest fixtures and fittings and the least room. However, it was relatively luxurious compared to the hard seats and cramped conditions of the earliest third-class compartments. Located over the wheels, its occupants had the most bumpy, noisy ride.

CARRIAGE KEYS
When carriages are not in use, they are usually locked for security. The lock is simple and operated by a square-shaped key.

THREE-IN-ONE
This 1904 carriage (below) is unusual in having first-, second-, and third-class accommodation in the same vehicle, with no connecting corridor. Each compartment had access to a lavatory. Because there was no corridor connecting this carriage to any other, it could be detached easily from the train.

First-class compartment

Second-class compartment

SECOND   6474

Travelling in style

Gold pass allowing directors and senior railway staff free first-class travel

By the 1850s, the railways of Europe and the USA were offering their passengers such luxurious facilities as heating, lighting, toilets, and catering, especially on long-distance trains. For the railway companies, the more luxury they offered, the more business they got. In the USA, businessman George Pullman introduced the first luxury sleeping cars in 1865 and went on to offer first-class dining facilities. Soon afterwards, railway companies with long-distance services started to build hotels alongside their main stations. From then on, the rapid spread of sleeping and dining cars, as well as railway hotels, made travelling by rail a stylish affair for wealthier passengers.

American Pullman train pass

French free pass

American free pass for Atchison, Topeka & Santa Fe railway

TOP-NOTCH TRAVELLERS
People such as railway directors who held free passes were able to travel first class at home as well as overseas.

CHINA AND ROSES
Trains with first-class dining cars would serve meals on fine china table settings, some of which have since become collectors' items. This breakfast setting was made in the 1930s and has a delicate gilt border with pink roses.

EXCLUSIVE EATING
To those who could afford it, the first-class restaurant car was just as enjoyable as an exclusive restaurant – with the added bonus of a constantly changing view.

TRAVEL A LA MODE
In the 1920s and 1930s the fashionable way to travel was by train. Striking images of elegant travellers from this period are sometimes still used by companies to promote their trains.

ANYONE FOR COCKTAILS?
Even cocktails could be ordered in first-class restaurant cars in Britain in the 1930s. Every railway company had their own monogram, which decorated glasses, silverware, and china.

WHODUNNIT? *left*
Famous luxury trains with romantic names have been the setting for many novels and films, including Agatha Christie's *Murder on the Orient Express*.

SYMBOL OF LUXURY *right*
The British Pullman Company coat of arms was carried on the exterior of all Pullman carriages. Pullman cars operated in Britain in one form or another from 1874 until the 1980s.

1960

Detailed marquetry (inlay) on wood-panelled walls

Bellpush for calling attendant

PULLMAN COMFORT
By the 1870s, American Pullman cars provided all that was needed for a long-distance journey. Travellers could even join in the Sunday hymns. Folded beds can be seen in the background.

PULLMAN STYLE
The interior of the 1914 Pullman car *Topaz* (left) reveals the ultimate in passenger comfort. British-built Pullman cars were renowned for their magnificent detailed woodwork (above). All the seats were armchairs, and each one had a glass-topped table and a brass table lamp in front of it, with a bellpush beside it for calling the attendant. Meals and refreshments were served at each seat. At each end of this car were private compartments holding four seats, known as coupés.

Oval lavatory window

Coupé door

Brass table lamp

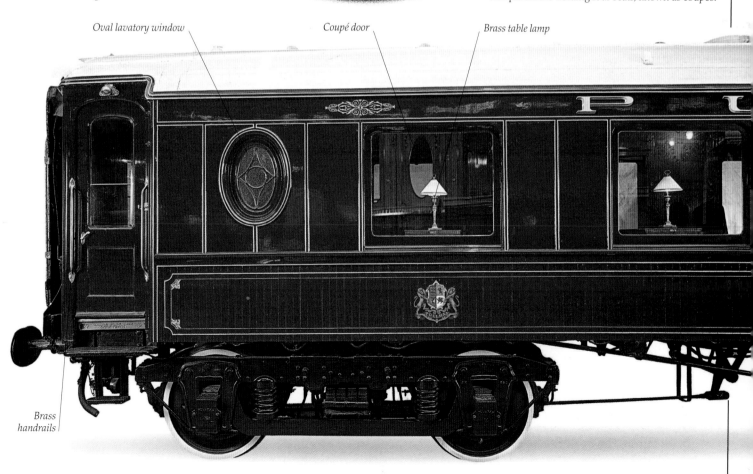

Brass handrails

In the signal box

THE SIGNAL BOX plays an important role in safe railway travel. In the early days, trains were prevented from crashing into each other by time intervals. People, waving flags or batons, signalled to trains when they could move. If a train had to change direction at a junction, the "points" were manually operated to switch the train to the right track. The invention of the electric telegraph, in the 1850s, enabled signalmen to send an electric bell code down the line. This development led to each train being separated by a space interval, called a "block". By this time, signals and points for each "block" were mechanically controlled from the signal box.

The signal box had an oil lamp in case of power failure

Bell sounds coded message from signal boxes on either side of this one

Yellow lever operates a distant (warning) signal

Two red levers for stop signals pulled into "off" or "clear" position

Blue levers control locks on points, black levers control points, and white levers are spare

WHAT'S WHAT?
This signal box has 40 levers in its frame for operating the signals and points. Above the lever frame are the various electrical instruments for sending and receiving signals from the signal boxes on either side of this box. Other instruments, called block instruments, indicate to the signalman whether the line in either direction is empty, or occupied by a train. To make these indicators failsafe, there are also precautionary "locks" between the instruments, signals, and the track. These ensure that trains are correctly signalled on the indicators, and that trains cannot be overlooked if they have broken down.

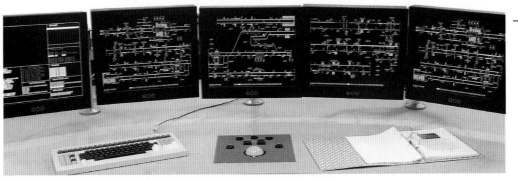

MODERN SIGNAL BOX
A modern signalling control centre (Dispatchers' Office) is programmed to run automatically unless there is a problem, such as a failed train, derailment, or broken signal. Then the signalman (Dispatcher) can intervene and set routes to deal with the problem and, crucially, keep the trains moving.

THREE-POSITION BLOCK INSTRUMENT
This instrument indicated to the signalman the state of the line between his box and the one before.

ON THE PLATFORM
At many smaller French stations the levers for signals and points were located behind barriers on the platform. This allowed the signalman to carry out other duties between signalling trains.

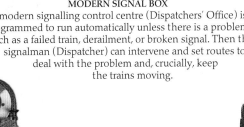

Single line electric key token instrument

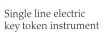

BELL TAPPER
If a signalman wanted to ask if the next section of line in advance was clear, he used this instrument to send bell codes to the boxes on either side of him.

ALL CLEAR
To operate the points and signals for each train passing through his block, the signalman had to pull the long levers that were linked to the points by rods, and to the signals by cables.

Staffs for a journey in the opposite direction were locked into the key token until the line was clear

THE SIGNAL BOX
Manually operated signal boxes in the early 1900s were often raised to accommodate the movement of the lower part of the levers. Today, one modern signal box can do the job of dozens of traditional signal boxes.

EXTRA PROTECTION
As an added safety measure, trains on single lines (for trains going in both directions) depended on key token instruments. A clear signal could be given to the driver only when he had been handed a metal staff, coded for the journey.

THREE-POSITION PEGGING BLOCK INSTRUMENT
This instrument sent information to the three-position block instrument in the signal box to the rear. It also displayed the state of the line.

Following the signs

TRAIN DRIVERS ARE FACED with an array of signals along the line. Without these, they risk colliding with other trains, as often happened in the early days of the railways. The first train drivers obeyed hand signals given by railway policemen. Later, mechanical signals imitated the same hand signals. As average train speeds rose and brakes improved, more sophisticated equipment was needed to improve the smoothness and safety of rail travel. By the 1920s, electric colour light signals for both day and night started to be used. These lights were much more powerful than the old oil lamps, and were much easier to see at a distance, especially at night on fast main lines. All high-speed main lines are now equipped with colour light signals which keep the driver informed about the state of the line ahead. These signals, and the points along the track, are all automatically indicated in the signal box.

STOP THE TRAIN!
At small rural stations, such as this one in Australia, the train only stopped if requested to do so. Passengers wanting to stop the train were told to "wave the tin flag".

Signalman's badge

IDENTIFICATION
Most people working on the railways have always worn badges as part of their uniform, to indicate who they are.

Red, square-ended arm is horizontal, meaning "stop"

STOP!
This mechanical semaphore signal has two arms. The upper arm indicates whether or not a train should stop, and the lower arm serves as a distant (warning) signal. It tells the driver to prepare to stop at the next signal. Here both signals are horizontal and indicate "stop".

SIGNALLING LAMP
In the past the guard would signal to the driver at the station by means of a flag during the day, and an oil lamp at night. The glass in this oil lamp could be rotated to give a green (go), red (stop), or white (general use) signal.

Three-aspect guard's lamp

BATONS AND ARMBAND
Early railway policemen, from around 1841, acted as signalmen. They would use different coloured flags to signal for a train to stop, proceed with caution, or to show that the line was all clear. They also wore armbands for clear identity, and ornately decorated truncheons at the waist in case they encountered trouble.

Road barrier – comes down across the road when train is due

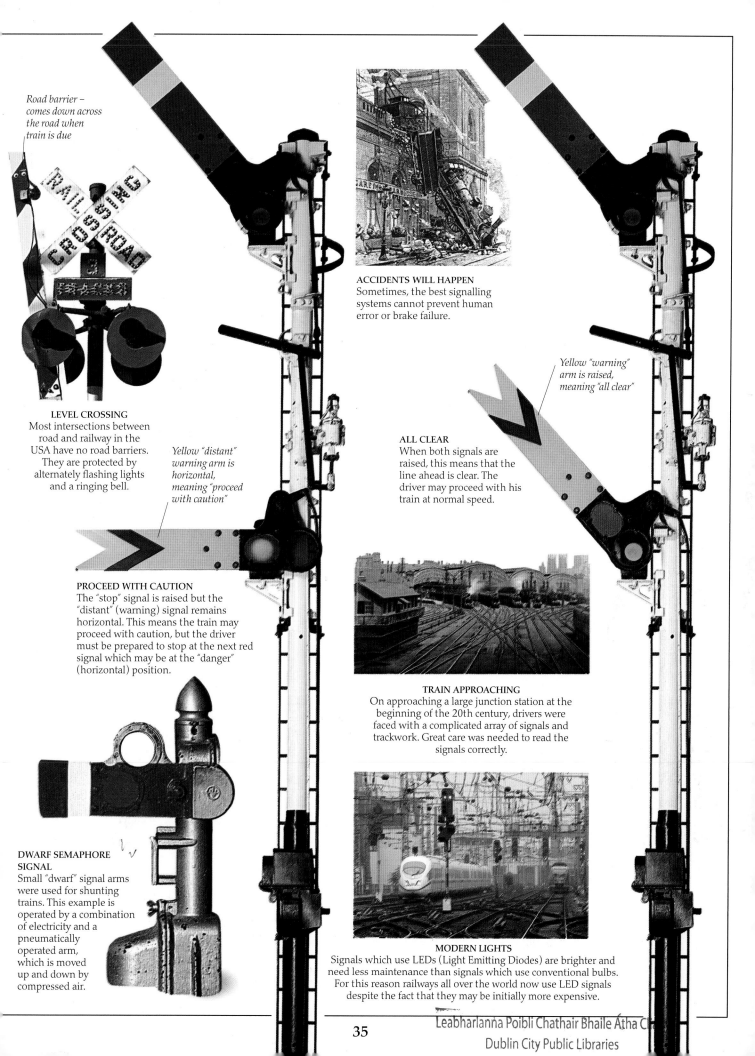

LEVEL CROSSING
Most intersections between road and railway in the USA have no road barriers. They are protected by alternately flashing lights and a ringing bell.

ACCIDENTS WILL HAPPEN
Sometimes, the best signalling systems cannot prevent human error or brake failure.

Yellow "distant" warning arm is horizontal, meaning "proceed with caution"

Yellow "warning" arm is raised, meaning "all clear"

ALL CLEAR
When both signals are raised, this means that the line ahead is clear. The driver may proceed with his train at normal speed.

PROCEED WITH CAUTION
The "stop" signal is raised but the "distant" (warning) signal remains horizontal. This means the train may proceed with caution, but the driver must be prepared to stop at the next red signal which may be at the "danger" (horizontal) position.

TRAIN APPROACHING
On approaching a large junction station at the beginning of the 20th century, drivers were faced with a complicated array of signals and trackwork. Great care was needed to read the signals correctly.

DWARF SEMAPHORE SIGNAL
Small "dwarf" signal arms were used for shunting trains. This example is operated by a combination of electricity and a pneumatically operated arm, which is moved up and down by compressed air.

MODERN LIGHTS
Signals which use LEDs (Light Emitting Diodes) are brighter and need less maintenance than signals which use conventional bulbs. For this reason railways all over the world now use LED signals despite the fact that they may be initially more expensive.

35

Post haste

THE TRAVELLING POST OFFICE VAN was designed to handle all the jobs that were carried out in a normal post office – while the train sped along. Without having to stop, the postal van could automatically pick up mail from specially designed lineside apparatus. It was then sorted and put into dispatch sacks for different destinations along the train's route. These sacks were automatically dropped off into lineside nets. The equipment for collecting and dropping off mail was located at one end of the vehicle, the rest of the van being devoted to sorting tables, pigeon-hole racks, and sacks for sorted mail.

PICKING UP
This cigarette card shows local mail, packaged in a leather bag, being picked up at speed by a long-distance Travelling Post Office train.

AMERICAN MAIL
This classic American locomotive from the 1870s is hauling a mail train. Mailbags are being thrown out for collection, while others prepare to collect a similar bag hanging from a post as the train passes by.

Post box for late letters. Letters posted here carried an extra fee

Mail to be collected by train

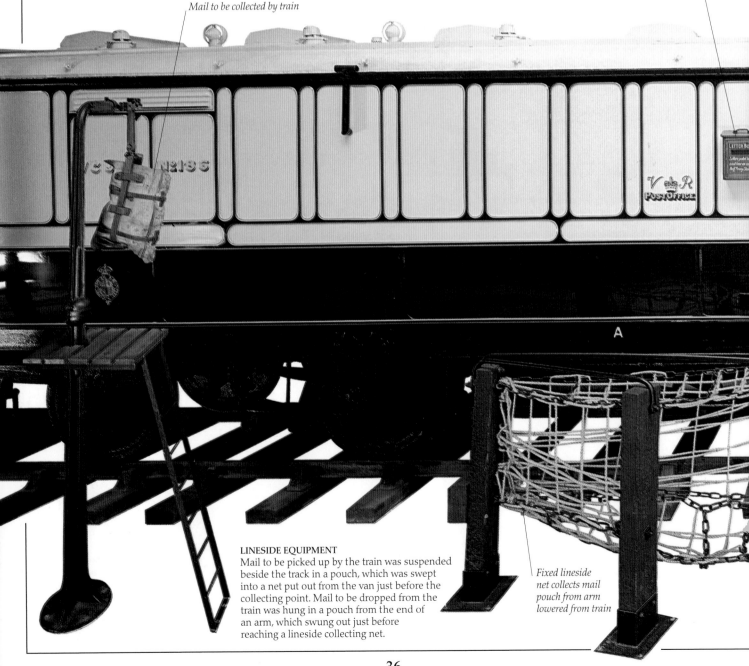

LINESIDE EQUIPMENT
Mail to be picked up by the train was suspended beside the track in a pouch, which was swept into a net put out from the van just before the collecting point. Mail to be dropped from the train was hung in a pouch from the end of an arm, which swung out just before reaching a lineside collecting net.

Fixed lineside net collects mail pouch from arm lowered from train

ROAD TO RAIL
Sending mail by rail requires cooperation between the railways and local postal services. Here, the mail van delivers mail to a branch-line station. The local train then takes the mail to a main-line station, where it is put aboard a long-distance passenger train or Travelling Post Office train.

SWIFTLY BY POST
The "Irish Mail" between London and Holyhead was the oldest named train in the world. It ran from 1848 until 1985, carrying mail from London en route to Dublin. The train also carried passengers, and sleeping accommodation was provided.

WHAT GOES WHERE?
Incoming mail was emptied from sacks onto the sorting table (left of picture), and individual letters were hand-sorted into pigeon-holes. When there were sufficient letters for one destination, they were tied in a bundle and put in a dispatch sack (right of picture). The sack was dropped off en route, or at the end of the journey.

Pigeon-holes for sorting letters

Net picks up mail bag from lineside

The apparatus for exchanging mail bags from a moving train was last used in 1971

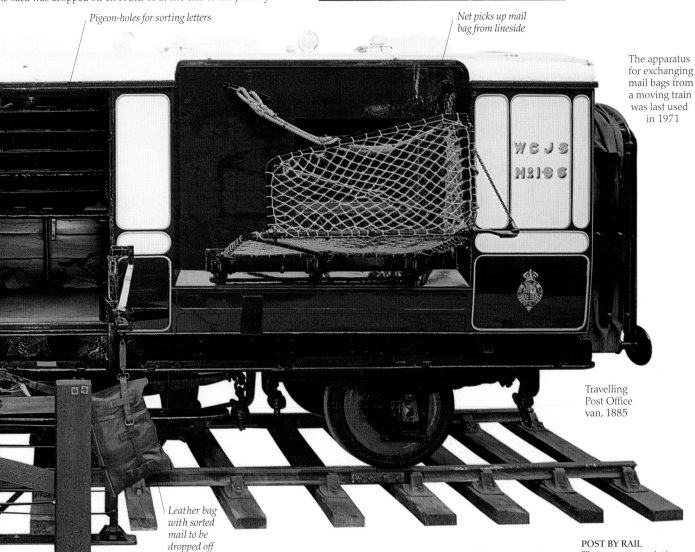

WC J S
N° 186

Travelling Post Office van, 1885

Leather bag with sorted mail to be dropped off

POST OFFICE ON WHEELS
In 1838, with the arrival of a regular railway passenger service in Britain, it was decided that the Royal Mail should be carried by rail, rather than by fast mail coaches. The railway postal service developed rapidly. In the USA, the first purpose-built railway Post Office car came into operation in 1864. The railways are still used today by mail services around the world, in conjunction with road and air transport.

POST BY RAIL
The strong association between trains and mail is illustrated by this 1974 Liberian postal stamp. The train is British Rail's "Experimental" Advanced Passenger Train which was retired in 1976.

Electric trains

THE POTENTIAL OF ELECTRIC POWER was understood in the early days of steam, but people had not yet worked out how to harness this power to drive trains. Engineers developed the first electric trains towards the end of the 19th century, and experimented with varying voltages of electric current. Some locomotives collected power from overhead cables, while others took power from a third "live" rail on the track. Electric locomotives have many advantages over steam and diesel power. They are faster, quieter, and easier to run. Although building an electric railway or electrifying an existing one is expensive, these lines are both economic and efficient and the extra costs are justified on busy lines such as the underground, rapid transit systems, and commuter services around the world.

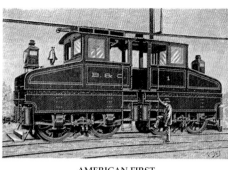

AMERICAN FIRST
The first electric locomotives to be used on an American main line were introduced on the Baltimore and Ohio Railroad in 1895 on a section of line 6 km (3.75 miles) long. This short route passed through many tunnels, which had easily filled with fumes when steam locomotives worked the line.

The pantograph is the "arm" on top of many electric locomotives and trains. It collects the electric current for the driving motors from the overhead power line

EARLY DAYS OF ELECTRICITY
The first practical electric railway was designed and operated in 1879 by German engineer Werner von Siemens, at an exhibition in Berlin. His locomotive could pull 30 passengers at a speed of 6.5 kph (4 mph).

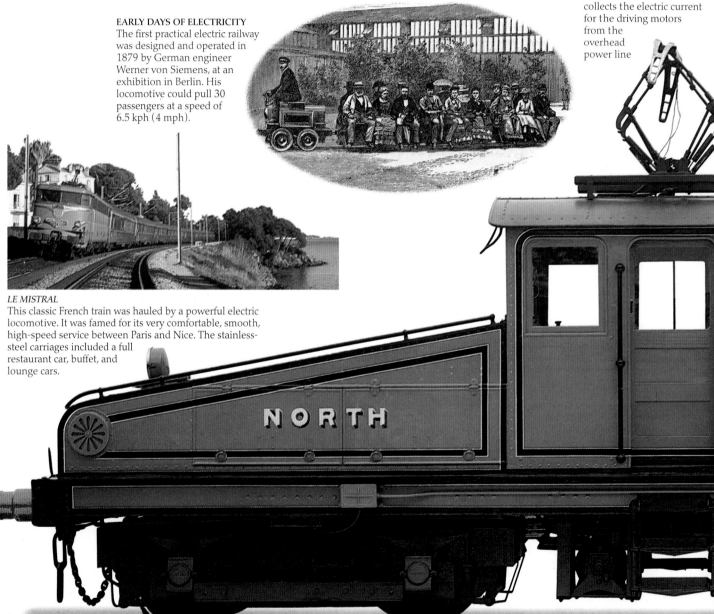

LE MISTRAL
This classic French train was hauled by a powerful electric locomotive. It was famed for its very comfortable, smooth, high-speed service between Paris and Nice. The stainless-steel carriages included a full restaurant car, buffet, and lounge cars.

NORTH

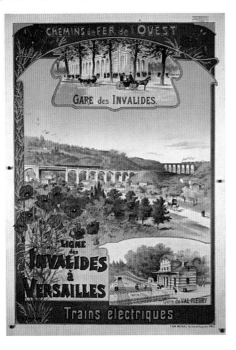

SWIFT AND SAFE
The French railways used eye-catching posters to advertise their new electric services in the early 1900s. This poster, in the art nouveau style, promoted the fast, clean electric trains running on a local service from Paris to Versailles.

VERY, VERY FAST
The fastest passenger train in the world is the TGV (*Train à Grande Vitesse*), a French high-speed electric train (pp. 46–47), which broke the World Rail Record in 2007 reaching 574.8 kph (357 mph). The orange TGV was the first one, introduced in 1981. It runs on tracks that were designed for the exclusive use of the train – they do not have slower passenger or freight trains on them. One TGV unit is made up of eight carriages with an electric locomotive at either end. Its modern design and powerful motors allow the TGV to maintain a high speed, even on steep gradients. This allowed tracks to be built over rather than through the landscape, so reducing construction and maintenance costs.

INNOVATIONS
Because of the rapid progress in electrical engineering, the latest designs for electric locomotives always run the risk of being superseded by better, more advanced designs. This 1991 electric locomotive works express trains on the electrified main line between London and Edinburgh, in Scotland. However, the carriages were designed with future developments in mind. They have sloping sides so that when tilting trains were later introduced (pp. 62–63), a major redesign was not necessary to keep trains clear of each other.

This electric locomotive was built in 1904 by the North Eastern Railway, England

EARLY ELECTRIC LOCOMOTIVE
This electric locomotive was built to replace steam locomotives on a freight line. The line had a badly ventilated tunnel which easily filled with choking fumes when worked by steam locomotives. The locomotive was designed to collect the electric current either by overhead pantograph or from a third "live" rail.

Diesel power

THE INVENTION OF THE diesel-powered locomotive, along with the electric locomotive, signalled that the age of steam was drawing to a close. The first diesel engine was demonstrated in 1893 by the German engineer Dr Rudolph Diesel, who went on to build the first reliable one in the world in 1897. In most diesel locomotives, the engine powers a generator which produces an electric current. This drives electric motors, which turn the wheels. Diesel-powered trains are used worldwide, particularly on less busy lines where electrification is not economical.

Rudolph Diesel

THE DIESEL ENGINE
Unlike a steam engine, a diesel engine does not usually drive the locomotive's wheels directly. Instead, it generates electricity which is used to turn the wheels. In the engine, heavy diesel oil is injected into a cylinder of hot, compressed air. The fuel ignites, and the energy released pushes a piston, which drives the generator. The generator makes electricity, which drives a motor that turns the wheels.

Fan cools generator

Generator produces an electric current, which is used to drive the wheels

Diesel engine drives generator

Prototype British Rail *Deltic* diesel-electric locomotive, 1956

40

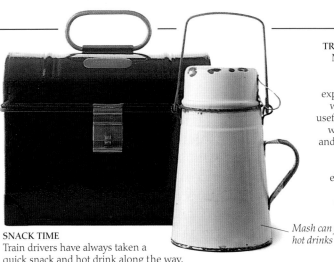

SNACK TIME
Train drivers have always taken a quick snack and hot drink along the way. The lunch box and mash can here are from the days of steam.

Mash can for hot drinks

TRANS-EUROP-EXPRESS
Major European cities were linked by an international luxury express service, the TEE, which was particularly useful for businesspeople wanting a fast, reliable, and comfortable intercity service. The self-contained diesel-electric trains on these lines only catered for first-class passengers.

Plastic top protects from grease and dirt

DIESEL RECORD
One of the first successful high-speed diesel trains was the *Zephyr* of the Burlington Route in the USA, introduced over the 1,609 km (1,000 mile) route from Chicago to Denver in the mid-1930s. In 1936, it set a start-to-stop average speed of 134 kph (83.3 mph), which is still a world record for a sustained rail speed on a run over 1,609 km (1,000 miles).

DRIVER'S CAP
Traditional steam-engine driver's caps like this were seen as a badge of seniority. They were also very useful in keeping soot and coal dust out of the hair.

TIME SAVER
High-speed diesel-electric trains, such as this British Rail High Speed Train, are designed to save time and labour. Instead of the traditional set of carriages hauled by a locomotive, the carriages travel between two diesel-electric power cars. At the end of the journey, the locomotive does not have to be replaced.

East German stamp featuring a diesel locomotive for shunting and local freight services

PROTOTYPE LOCOMOTIVE
When this *Deltic* diesel-electric locomotive was built in 1956, it was the most powerful diesel-electric single-unit locomotive in the world. The *Deltics* successfully replaced the powerful streamlined steam locomotives of the *Mallard* type (pp. 46–47) on the East Coast main line between London and Edinburgh in 1961. In the 20 years that they worked this line, they each ran more than three million miles. Diesel-electric locomotives have proved to be far more powerful than the steam locomotives that preceded them.

Long distance by train

Whole continents were opened up by the building of long-distance railways. Early journeys on such railways were often slow and uncomfortable. But they were an improvement on what, if anything, had been available before. The facilities on long-distance trains slowly improved, specially in the USA, with heating, special carriages for sleeping, and eventually restaurant cars being introduced. Today, most businesspeople fly on longer journeys to save time. Long-distance trains, however, remain increasingly popular with tourists. For those who are not in a hurry, travelling by train is an excellent way to see much of a country.

Early sleeping cars had flexible curtains, allowing complete privacy

TRANS-SIBERIAN EXPRESS
The passenger train between Moscow and Vladivostock – *The Russia* – makes one of the longest regular train journeys in the world, 9,297 km (5,778 miles), taking eight days in all.

STRAIGHT AND NARROW
The first through-running service from Sydney on the east coast of Australia to Perth on the west coast was introduced in 1970. The luxury *Indian Pacific* train covers the 3,968 km (2,461 mile) route, including the world's longest length of straight track – 478 km (297 miles) – in three days.

BLUE TRAIN
A luxury train has run between Cape Town and Pretoria in South Africa since 1903. In 1939, the *Blue Train* was introduced on this 1,540-km (956-mile) stretch, and is now regarded as the most luxurious train in the world.

Containers for tea and coffee

Kettle

Saucepan

Paraffin burner

SNACK TIME
As train speeds increased, station stops for refreshments were greatly reduced, or abandoned altogether. Passengers took to bringing their own food in luncheon baskets, such as this one containing tea-making equipment. Self-catering on trains remained popular even after the introduction of restaurant cars in 1879.

Strap prevented occupant of upper berth falling out during stormy night passages

Rack for luggage and bedding when bed is folded up

Cupboard containing bottle of drinking water and glass

When covered, washbasin makes a small table

Toilets and washbasins were provided on sleeping cars

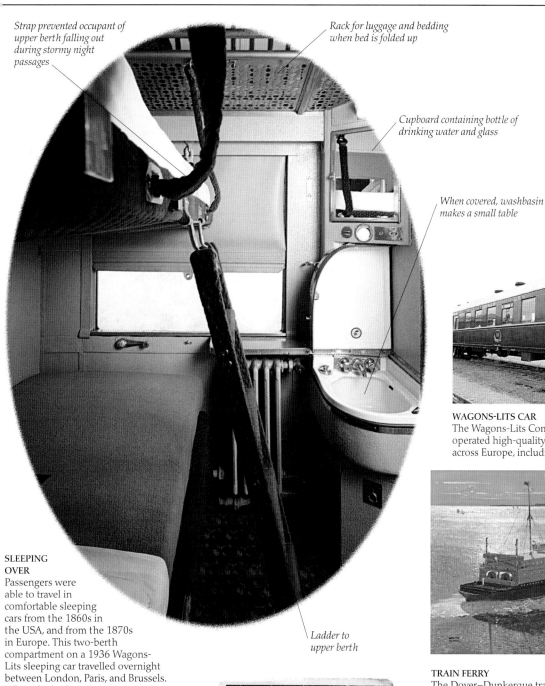

Ladder to upper berth

SLEEPING OVER
Passengers were able to travel in comfortable sleeping cars from the 1860s in the USA, and from the 1870s in Europe. This two-berth compartment on a 1936 Wagons-Lits sleeping car travelled overnight between London, Paris, and Brussels. When the beds were not in use, the lower berth was converted into seats. Trains on this route crossed the English Channel on board a train-ferry.

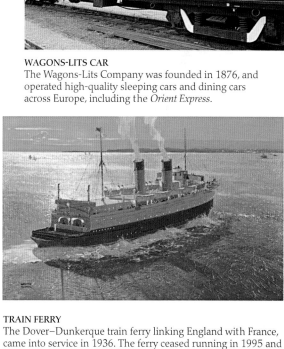

WAGONS-LITS CAR
The Wagons-Lits Company was founded in 1876, and operated high-quality sleeping cars and dining cars across Europe, including the *Orient Express*.

TRAIN FERRY
The Dover–Dunkerque train ferry linking England with France, came into service in 1936. The ferry ceased running in 1995 and all freight traffic now goes by lorry or via the Channel Tunnel. Train ferries for passenger carriages do still run but are rare.

Eating lunch in the dining car

Super Chief ticket of 1938

SUPER SERVICE
The *Super Chief* service travelled between Chicago and Los Angeles in the USA. It established, with the help of gourmet food and a Hollywood clientele, a reputation as the best long-distance train in the USA.

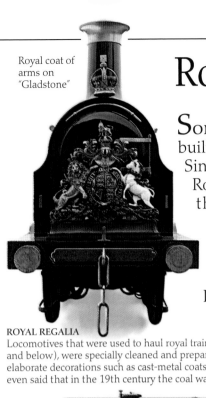

Royal trains

SOME OF THE MOST SPLENDID railway carriages ever built were constructed for the British Royal Family. Since the first royal railway journey in 1839, the Royal Family have travelled by train when making their longer civic and family journeys around Britain. The railways offered greater comfort, space, and privacy than road transport. When built, the royal carriages represented the latest in design, furnishing, and technology. Royal trains are still used today.

GLADSTONE'S LAMP
Oil head-lamps on locomotives pulling royal trains were often decorated like this example from *Gladstone*.

ROYAL REGALIA
Locomotives that were used to haul royal trains, like *Gladstone* (above and below), were specially cleaned and prepared. They usually carried elaborate decorations such as cast-metal coats of arms and flags. It is even said that in the 19th century the coal was painted white!

By day the Queen sat in the coupé compartment, which had end windows

Attendants' compartment

ROYAL STATIONS
Queen Victoria was a regular train traveller and made many civic visits by railway. Some stations were built especially for royal use, such as this one at Gosport, which the Queen used when travelling to her residence on the Isle of Wight. The station was richly decorated for her arrival, and she was always greeted with pomp and ceremony.

No 2

QUEEN ADELAIDE'S CARRIAGE
The first royal saloon was made for the Dowager Queen Adelaide in 1842. The design was based on three stagecoach compartments, and was the state of the art in the field of carriage construction at the time. The interior was beautifully furnished and upholstered by craftsmen. It is thought that the Queen travelled during the day in the end (or coupé) compartment, with close attendants in the middle compartment.

QUEEN VICTORIA'S LAVATORY
Much attention was paid to the smallest of rooms. This toilet and washing compartment was beautifully furnished in maple and silk.

QUEEN VICTORIA'S DAY SALOON *above*
No expense was spared when fitting out the royal carriages. The decoration of the day saloon was the personal choice of the Queen when it was built in 1869. The wood is bird's-eye maple, the upholstery is blue watered silk, and the ceilings are covered in white quilted silk. The saloon was originally lit with oil lamps, but in 1895 newly developed electric lighting and bells for calling attendants were added. It is said that the Queen preferred oil lamps and specially requested that they be kept as well.

KING EDWARD VII'S SMOKING COMPARTMENT
Edward liked to relax in this wood-panelled compartment in his 1902 saloon. It contained the latest electric fans, heaters, and even cigar-lighters.

QUEEN ALEXANDRA'S BEDROOM
On the wall above the Queen's bed were a number of buttons. She could use these to summon any of her servants to her royal bedside during the night.

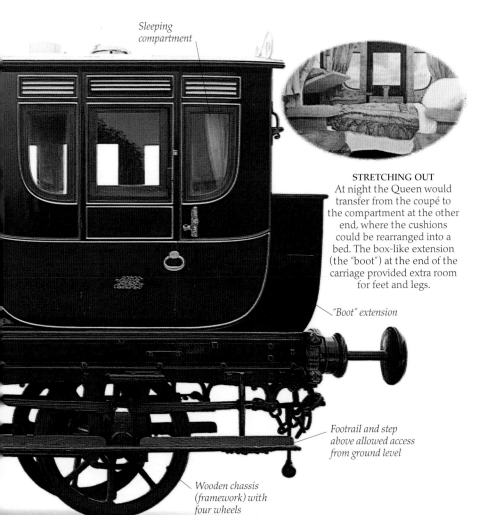

Sleeping compartment

STRETCHING OUT
At night the Queen would transfer from the coupé to the compartment at the other end, where the cushions could be rearranged into a bed. The box-like extension (the "boot") at the end of the carriage provided extra room for feet and legs.

"Boot" extension

Footrail and step above allowed access from ground level

Wooden chassis (framework) with four wheels

QUEEN MARY'S DAY COMPARTMENT
The day compartment was one of several compartments in the Queen's saloon. She also had a dressing room, bathroom, and bedroom.

Record breakers

RAILWAYS HAVE OFTEN been involved with spectacle, publicity, and competition – especially in setting speed records. For Britain and the USA, breaking the speed barrier of one hundred miles per hour was a special target. This target was reputedly met in 1893, when an American locomotive was claimed to have reached a speed of 181 kph (112.5 mph), and in 1904, when a British locomotive was timed at 164 kph (102 mph). However, serious doubts were subsequently cast on both these claims. From the early days of steam right up to the present day, speed records have been, and still are being, set and broken as countries compete for the absolute record for a standard train.

FAST MOVERS
The first steam engines designed to run at 161 kph (100 mph) on every trip were those of the 1935 *Hiawatha* service, covering 663 km (412 miles) between Chicago and Minneapolis/St Paul. The service holds the world record for the fastest-ever run between two stations on a scheduled service with steam power–it averaged 130 kph (80 mph) over a 127 km (78.9 mile) stretch.

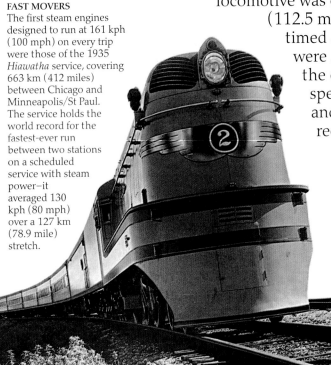

Steam train of the *Hiawatha* service

THE BEST EVER
The brass plaque attached to the side of the boiler of *Mallard* commemorates the world speed record for a steam locomotive set on 3 July, 1938.

Mallard is a streamlined Pacific-type steam locomotive built by the London North Eastern Railway at Doncaster in 1938

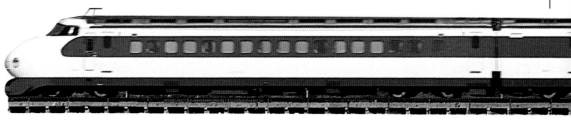

LIKE A BULLET
When opened in 1964, the Japanese electric Shinkansen, or "new high-speed railway", between Tokyo and Osaka was the first in the world of a new generation of high-speed railways built exclusively for intercity passenger trains.

The first regular Shinkansen service, in 1965, travelled at an average speed of 163 kph (101 mph), with a maximum of 210 kph (130 mph)

INTERCITY EXPRESS
This German electric high-speed train was introduced on a number of services in 1991. The ICE mainly runs on upgraded existing lines, although special high-speed tracks are also used. During tests on these high-speed lines, the ICE set a German high-speed record of 404 kph (252 mph), which was a world record for a short time.

LOCOMOTIVE NO. 999
In 1893 the New York Central Railroad claimed that its steam locomotive No. 999 had become the first to exceed 161 kph (100 mph), when it reached 181 kph (112.5 mph) while working the *Empire State Express* near Batavia, New York. However, this record is no longer recognized internationally.

THE FASTEST EVER
The TGV (*Train à Grande Vitesse*), a French electric high-speed train, was introduced in 1981 between Paris and Lyon and extended over the years. TGVs run on specially designed tracks in the country travelling at up to 320 kph (200 mph) and join the standard railway near their destination to access existing stations. In 2007, a modified TGV achieved a world record of 574.8 kph (357 mph) on the new Paris to Strasbourg LGV line.

STEAM RECORD
The streamlined locomotive *Mallard* was designed by British engineer Sir Nigel Gresley. On 3 July, 1938, *Mallard* set a world speed record for a steam locomotive of 203 kph (126 mph). It was pulling a special train, including a speed-recording car, down a gradient on the main line between London and Edinburgh. This record still stands.

At the station

THE FIRST STATIONS were little more than a wooden shelter next to the rails and platforms. Passengers were able to buy tickets and wait for the train there, as well as get on and off the train. Today, some small rural stations are still very simple buildings, providing little more than a ticket counter and a waiting room. But where the railway station is in a major town or city, services offered range from porters for luggage, refreshment rooms, and car parks, to links with road and other rail transport. Very often, the station is the largest building in town, built on a grand scale, with imposing architecture in styles from all ages, from classical to ultra-modern.

A large clock is often the focal point of a station

RAILWAY TIME
For a railway to operate successfully, trains must run to time. In the early days, countries with a large east-west spread, like the USA, presented timekeeping problems. Eventually, these countries were divided into different time zones, so the time changes whenever a train crosses into a new zone.

COUNTRY STATION
Simple stations in rural areas often have a very low platform, or none at all. Passengers enter or leave the train by climbing onto steps on the carriages. Road wagons reverse up to the freight cars, or use the low platform to load and unload.

TRANSPORT FOR ALL
Before road and air transport had developed, the railways were used for transporting all kinds of goods. This enclosed trolley was used for coffins.

GRAND CENTRAL STATION
Information boards on the station concourse show passengers where and when trains are arriving and departing. New York's Grand Central Station, the largest station in the world, has a huge cavernous concourse.

Late 19th-century pocket watch

Simple metal whistle

WHISTLE STOP
Simple whistles made from wood or metal were used by platform staff for communication, usually to tell the driver when a train was ready for departure.

Railway uniform button forms part of this whistle

WATERLOO STATION
Large stations are designed so that hundreds – or even thousands – of travellers can quickly board or leave their train, all at the same time, during peak hours.

TIME IN HAND
The operation of trains to a strict timetable meant that key staff, as well as stations, had to have an accurate timepiece. Stations had large clocks, and railway staff were provided with fob watches.

Japanese railway tickets

SOUTHERN RAILWAY PARCEL DELIVERY SERVICE FROM HORSTED KEYNES STATION

SPECIAL DELIVERY
In the 1920s and 1930s the railways provided a complete transport service, ferrying freight to and from stations using their own road vehicles. Bicycles were used for delivering small parcels locally.

LANDMARKS
Major stations, such as the *Gare de Lyon* in Paris, were designed to provide easy access for road traffic bringing freight and passengers. Their imposing architecture made such stations a familiar landmark.

LISTEN FOR THE BELL
Handbells were rung to announce the arrival of a train in the days before electricity was available to operate electric bells.

London, Chatham and Dover Railway insignia

A first-class ticket to Basra in Iraq

THE ROMANCE OF STEAM
The days of steam are often portrayed as a romantic age. The classic film *Brief Encounter* is based on a chance meeting at a railway station shortly after World War II.

TICKETS PLEASE!
All around the world, passengers have to buy a ticket for their journey. Tickets are proof that a passenger has paid their fare. A ticket inspector marks the ticket with a clipper so that it cannot be used again.

Running the railway

British porter's cap badge

OILING THE WHEELS
Steam train drivers were responsible for checking that their locomotive was in working order.

IN ADDITION TO THE FAMILIAR FACES of the station and train staff, many more people are required to run a railway. At the centre of railway activities are the commercial departments. In liaison with top management, they specify the type, frequency, and speed of passenger and freight trains needed. It is then the job of the operating department to meet these demands. The technical engineering department must provide the necessary equipment, while the civil engineering team ensures that the track and fixed structures are in working order. All this work is supported by many specialised departments, ranging from timetabling and accounts to marketing and publicity.

Russian railway worker's badge

Chinese railway worker's badge

Signalman
Fireman
Porter
Ticket inspector
Waiter
Chef
Engine driver
Shunter
Porter
Station master
Guard

SMOOTH OPERATION
The railways need a wide variety of workers in order to run smoothly. For this reason, the railways have traditionally been among the biggest employers in many countries.

Station-masters are now known as area managers, and are responsible for a number of stations

Great Western Railway fireman's helmet

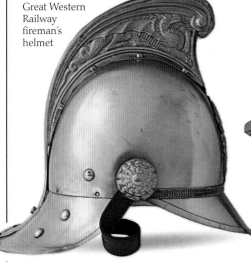

SAFETY FIRST
The railways ran their own fire service, trained to deal with any special hazards which might arise. The service had its own equipment and uniform.

TRAVELLERS' HELPER
In the past, railway companies owned many of the station hotels in big cities or at major junctions. The hotel porter assisted passengers arriving or departing from the hotel.

STATION-MASTER
The station-master had an important role. He was in charge of all aspects of running his station and had to ensure that trains arrived and departed promptly.

When the horn was blown, the men stepped clear of the track and waited for the train to pass

This horn sounded a distinctive note that could not be confused with a guard's whistle

Look-out man's brass horn

The railway track was known as "the permanent way"

INDISPENSABLE
Even today, with modern electrical equipment, the signal engineer has an important role, especially on busy lines. However, all signal equipment is designed to be "fail-safe" by displaying red stop signals if it fails to work.

The hose is fitted into the dining car's water tank

THE PERMANENT WAY
A great deal of organisation and effort went – and still goes – into maintaining the railway track so that trains could make a safe and smooth journey. The look-out man, in charge of the working team, would blow the horn to warn them of an approaching train.

TOPPING UP
In the short time that a long-distance express train stood at a station, it would have to be stocked up with enough food and water to last until the next refuelling stop. This water carrier was used to replenish the tanks for drinking water in dining cars. The tanks for the lavatories would be refilled using hoses linked to local water supplies.

When the wheel turns, it pumps water through the hose

TOOLS OF THE TRADE
This oil-can was designed for filling oil lamps. The broad base makes it difficult to knock over.

Oil can from around 1890

Thick, multi-stranded wick

LIGHTING UP
Flare lamps provided light before electric battery lamps were introduced. Oil was kept in the body of the lamp, and was burned at the end of the wick. The lamp warned of hazards in yards, as well as being used for inspecting steam locomotives.

Oil flare lamp from around 1900

The water carrier is wheeled along the platform

Still in steam

NOWADAYS, steam locomotives still operate in a handful of places on ordinary trains, particularly in heavy industry and especially in Asia. In most parts of the world the days of the steam locomotive are a thing of the past. Cleaner, more efficient diesel and electric power have taken their place. However, plans exist to build more efficient and modern steam locomotives and some have recently been built for service on tourist lines in Switzerland. Elsewhere, the enthusiasm for steam locomotives has kept them alive. Hundreds of steam locomotives throughout the world are owned by private railway preservation societies and transport museums, and many have been carefully restored to working order. They are used to pull trains on preserved lines, or on the quieter scenic lines of the national railway networks, for tourists and enthusiasts.

KEEPING ON TRACK
Until recently steam trains still worked the main lines in India. Most narrow gauge locomotives, such as this one from India's South Eastern Railway, were imported to India from France, Germany, and Japan.

STAR EXHIBIT
Evening Star was the last steam locomotive built for British Rail in 1960. It was intended for freight work, but also pulled passenger and express trains in the 1960s. It was withdrawn from service in 1966, and is on display in Britain's National Railway Museum in York.

TOURIST ATTRACTIONS
Nowadays, many steam railways are tourist attractions. Some, such as the narrow gauge Llanberis Lake Railway in Wales (above), are modelled on working railways that no longer exist. Others use the original routes of old railways.

PRESERVED STEAM

The USA was quick to turn from steam power to electric and diesel power. There are, however, an increasing number of steam locomotives preserved in working order. Train enthusiasts can ride on some of the spectacular main-line classic routes, or on local lines. Steam locomotives are also demonstrated at museums or private steam centres.

The building of new steam locomotives in China only ceased at the end of the 1980s

Preserved locomotive of Fort Worth & Western Railroad

LONG LIVE STEAM

Railways form the backbone of public transport in China. At the beginning of 1990 there were some 7,000 steam locomotives, compared with 4,700 diesel and 1,200 electric. Now, only a few steam locomotives still run on industrial lines.

ZIMBABWE'S STEAM REVIVAL

In the late 1970s, Zimbabwe Railways refurbished a number of their British-built Beyer-Garratt steam locomotives. This was due to the plentiful supply of Zimbabwe coal, and the wish to be independent of expensive imported oil used to fuel diesel locomotives. For this reason, Zimbabwe has attracted railway enthusiasts from all over the world, to see and photograph one of the most powerful working steam locomotives in existence.

VETERAN LOCOMOTIVES

Although most steam locomotives were taken off main railway lines in India and Pakistan a decade ago, there are still a few tourist steam trains operating there, and locomotives, such as an old British tank engine, attract enthusiasts from all over the world.

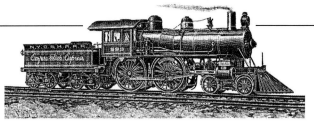

All decked out

Rᴀɪʟᴡᴀʏs ᴡᴇʀᴇ ᴇsᴛᴀʙʟɪsʜᴇᴅ in the 19th century, an age familiar with elaborate decoration, so it is not surprising that they too, were highly decorated. Imaginative displays helped to promote the services the railway provided. Colourful signs on tunnel entrances and decorated stations also reassured the public, who were not familiar with travelling by rail. As competition grew between the different railway companies, decorations sporting the name of the company were applied to most railway property, large and small. These decorations were often in the form of a coat of arms or a monogram of the company's initials. Huge, colourful cast-iron plaques were hung on railway bridges, and company initials were even to be found on the heads of copper nails for slate tiles.

COAT OF ARMS
The ornate coat of arms of the Midland Railway featured a winged monster, as well as the emblems of the major cities served by the railway.

TGV NAMEPLATE
Many of the French TGV trains' powercar units are named after cities served by these trains.

EXPRESS TRAIN HEADBOARD
The headboard displayed the name of the train. It was fastened in front of the chimney of the steam locomotive hauling the train.

UNIQUE TRAINS
Locomotives working special trains were often decorated with badges or headboards created just for the occasion.

LION CREST
This crest was displayed on British Railways locomotives and carriages during the 1950s.

American works plate

Southern Railway nameplate

WORKS PLATE
Most locomotives carry a works plate which gives the building number and date, as well as the name, and very often the location of the building company. This plate also carries the name of the company's president.

FAMOUS NAMES
Many locomotives have carried names of one kind or another. These ranged from classical figures through famous figures of all kinds to directors of the railway and names of places served by the railway.

BRASS NAMEPLATE
This cast brass nameplate was one of several that commemorated links with the British Commonwealth.

London and North Eastern Railway nameplate

DOMINION OF NEW ZEALAND

KNIGHT OF·THE GOLDEN FLEECE

KNIGHT OF THE GOLDEN FLEECE
This classical name was carried by an express locomotive of the Great Western Railway.

The crown indicates that the railway was the only one in Canada operated with Royal Charter

The headboard carried the name of the service

GOLD COAST RAILWAY
The coat of arms of the Gold Coast Railway featured an elephant, a familiar sight in this West African country, now known as Ghana.

DOMINION ATLANTIC RAILWAY. 39

NUMBER PLATE
This brass number plate is from a 1902 locomotive belonging to the Canadian Dominion Atlantic Railway.

WHAT GOES WHERE?
The headboard and nameplate were carried on the locomotive. The railway company's coat of arms was displayed on the locomotive and on the carriages.

CITY OF MANCHESTER

GOOD PUBLICITY
Locomotives were, and still are, named after towns and cities served by the railway, as seen in this nameplate carried by a London Midland and Scottish Railway locomotive.

Scottish flag

English flag

CALEDONIAN HEADBOARD
The shields on this headboard carry motifs of the flags of England and Scotland.

THE CALEDONIAN

LOCAL WILDLIFE
Railway coats of arms often included images of local interest. A black swan was the symbol of the Western Australian Government Railways from 1890 to 1976.

Travelling underground

THE SUCCESS OF THE RAILWAYS in bringing people and business to large cities also led to congestion in the streets. In London this led to the building of the world's first underground railway in 1863, connecting the main line station of Paddington to Farringdon Street. This steam-powered railway, which ran just below the streets, was built using the cut and cover system (by digging a trench and then covering it to form a tunnel). Despite the smoky atmosphere, it was quicker and more convenient than road travel. Later developments, such as ways of digging deeper tunnels, electric locomotives, better lifts, and escalators, allowed routes to be built deep beneath the centre of London. The system became known as the "tube". The great advantages of electric underground railways encouraged other cities around the world to develop their own systems. "Tubes" continue to be built – and existing lines extended – in Beijing, China, the new Line 5 opened in 2007.

DRIVERLESS TRAINS?
Most modern rapid transit systems, such as the Metro in Washington D.C., are ideal for automation. This is because they have a steady flow of traffic and there is no disruption by slower freight trains or faster express services. The entire network is run by a central computer-based control system, and the trains need no drivers.

LUXURY FOR ALL
The first underground railway in Moscow opened in 1933. The imposing stations were famed for their luxurious decor.

OIL HAND LAMP
Hand lamps similar to this one have been used by guards and signalmen for many years.

EARLY DAYS
Early impressions of the first underground steam railway show trains travelling through spacious tunnels, into which some natural light filtered. In reality, the smoke and fumes made travelling by underground train dirty and unpleasant.

Water tank

The train driver stood here

METROPOLITAN 23 RAILWAY.

Guard rail keeps track clear of small obstacles

ALL PACKED IN
Underground carriages have automatic sliding doors and wide gangways to provide as much space as possible for commuters, both seated and standing.

UNIFORM BADGE
Striking badges worn as part of their uniform make underground railway staff easily recognisable.

London Transport badge with heraldic griffins, from early 1930s

PARIS METRO
The underground railway opened in Paris in 1900, and was called the *Metro*. *Metro* stations are very close together and easily recognisable by their signs. Any point in the city centre is within comfortable walking distance of a station.

READING THE MAP
Some underground systems, such as the Paris Metro, carefully relate the route of the lines to the streets above them. This example of a London Underground map of 1927 is roughly based on a geographical map of London. Maps used today make no attempt to do this, and are not to scale.

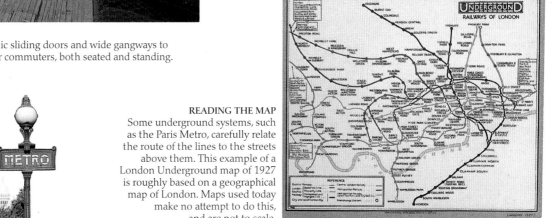

WHERE ARE WE?
Japan's underground railway, which opened in Tokyo in 1927, is now a large and very busy system. This Tokyo subway ticket has a route map on one side.

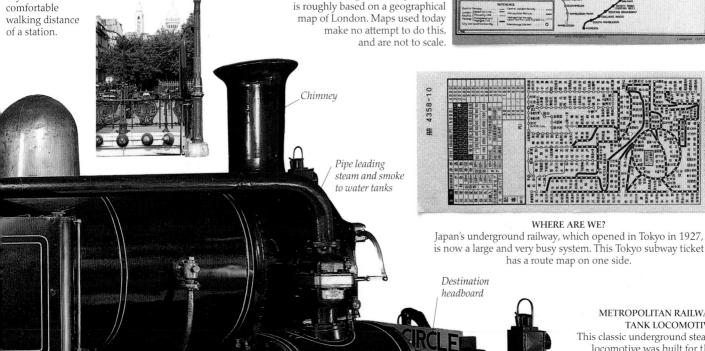

Chimney

Pipe leading steam and smoke to water tanks

Destination headboard

CIRCLE

METROPOLITAN RAILWAY TANK LOCOMOTIVE
This classic underground steam locomotive was built for the Metropolitan Railway in London in 1866, only three years after the underground railway opened. To reduce the emission of smoke and steam while working in the tunnels, this locomotive was fitted with a valve to divert smoke and steam into its water tanks. The tanks acted as condensers, stopping the smoke and steam from blowing straight up the chimney and overpowering passengers. Unfortunately, this technique slowed down the locomotive. To make up for lost time, drivers did not always operate the condensing equipment in the tunnels. Conditions could become very unpleasant, especially in the rush hours.

Up in the air

SOME RAILWAYS DO NOT RUN ALONG the ground, as conventional railways do. Instead, they run on or hang underneath rails fixed to overhead structures. There are two such types of railway: suspended railways, where the train hangs under a rail or rails, or "straddle" railways, where the train fits over a single rail. Suspended trains have wheels that are securely fitted onto the rails, and there is no risk of the trains falling to the ground. Trains running on the "straddle" system rest astride a single rail, and are balanced and guided by side panels on either side of the rail. Overhead systems with a single rail are called monorails. The idea of having overhead railways is not a new one. Several major cities in Europe and the USA operated elevated railways (conventional railways running on overhead tracks) by the end of the 19th century, and a monorail has been used in Germany since 1901. Modern overhead railways are less expensive to build than conventional railways. They offer passengers a good view, and avoid conflict with ground traffic, something neither conventional rail or road systems can offer. Like conventional electric trains, modern overhead trains do not pollute the air. They are, however, very prominent and many consider them to be an eyesore, as well as being noisier than street trains due to their elevated position.

NEW YORK'S ELEVATED RAILWAY
Towards the end of the 19th century, as street congestion in large cities grew, elevated railways were seen as a cheaper and more flexible alternative to underground railways. This elevated city railway was built in New York in the 1880s.

Second track for cars going in opposite direction

MONTMARTRE FUNICULAR
Funicular railways are a form of cable railway, used for raising or lowering loads on steep ground over relatively short distances. They were originally developed with a double track for freight work. The cable system was balanced so that loaded wagons descending on one line helped to pull up empty or partly laden wagons on the adjacent line. Most funiculars are now electrically powered, and carry passengers rather than freight. The cars are attached to a common cable, and neither can move until both ascending and descending trains are ready. This funicular line in Montmartre, Paris, was built in 1900, and is still operating today with new cars.

OUT OF THE WAY
The compact and flexible nature of a monorail system makes it ideal for a wide variety of uses. Monorails, such as this one at the National Motor Museum at Beaulieu, England, have often been used to transport visitors around exhibitions and leisure parks. Because they are elevated, these railways can cover ground crowded with pedestrians without causing any obstruction.

ERECTED OVER
L·N·E·R LINE—
MILNGAVIE STATION
(NEAR GLASGOW)

NOVELTY VALUE
Monorails have great novelty value and are frequently used in leisure parks. This small lightweight open-car monorail operates in a Dutch zoo, where animals may be viewed and photographed in complete safety.

GLASGOW SAIL PLANE
This sail plane was developed in the 1920s by George Bennie and tried out near Glasgow, in Scotland. It was a suspended monorail that travelled along the track using a propeller similar to those used on aeroplanes. The motor to drive the propeller could be either diesel or electric. Despite the usual advantages of an overhead railway, the sail plane was not developed beyond the experimental stage.

THE FIRST MONORAIL
The first commercial monorail opened in Wuppertal, northwest Germany, in 1901 and is still in operation today. The electric trains are suspended beneath the rail. For much of its 12.9-km (8-mile) journey, the railway straddles the river Wupper.

Monorails travel on a single rail, or beam

Power line

Side web of rail

TRAIN WITH ONE RAIL
Most modern monorails, such as this one (exhibited in Brisbane, Australia at the Expo '88 fair), are designed so that the car straddles the supporting structure. It is balanced and guided by side panels which contain guide wheels. The car runs on electric power, which is collected from conductor strips set in the side webs of the rail, or beam. Monorails are also used in permanent locations – the train from Tokyo to Haneda Airport, Japan, a distance of 13 km (8 miles) is a monorail.

Supporting beam

Trains for fun

No sooner had railways been invented for transport than people began to build them, in one form or the other, for amusement. These ranged from simple toy trains for children to push on the floor to complex scaled-down versions of full-size trains. The earliest toy trains, made of flat pieces of lead, were followed by wooden trains with rotating wheels. By the latter half of the 19th century, wooden models had given way to tin-plate trains running on model tracks, driven at first by clockwork and later by electricity. As manufacturing techniques improved, models became more detailed to satisfy the demand for greater accuracy. The traditional children's toy increasingly became the more sophisticated miniature scale model of the enthusiast and collector. But, whether simple toys or miniature scale models, trains still fascinate children and adults alike.

Brake van   Milk van

These images are cut out and made into three-dimensional locomotives

CUT AND PASTE
Miniature cardboard cutout "do-it-yourself" models are an alternative and cheaper way of collecting models of famous locomotives. This example was promoted as "a workshop in a cigar box".

SMALLER THAN LIFE
Miniature railways on which children and adults can ride are built just for entertainment. They have been popular since the 19th century, especially when pulled by steam.

GRAND JUNCTION RAILWAY LOCOMOTIVE
This precision-engineered model is of a classic freight locomotive design dating from 1846. A good model of this sort has all the features of a full-size train in working order – such as oil lamps, levers, and whistles.

THE PERFECT PRESENT
Train sets have always made ideal gifts for children of all ages. A basic train set can be built up to include stations, bridges, tunnels, signals, and all the elements of a modern railway.

1930s freight train set

TIN-PLATE TRAINS
British tin-plate clockwork train sets were well-made and reasonably durable. Such sets included lengths of track and sometimes other accessories, such as points, stations, and tunnels.

Tanker wagon   Cement wagon

PRECISION-MADE MODEL
Models are often made of famous locomotives, such as this mass-produced but detailed model of a heavy freight steam locomotive built in the early 1940s for America's Union Pacific Railroad. Although this model uses mostly metal materials, well-moulded plastics are more often used today to provide more accurate detail and to reduce costs.

BOARD GAMES
The railways had such a huge impact on society that the railway theme appeared in many aspects of everyday life. Even family games, such as this French board game of the 1870s, featured the railways.

THOMAS THE TANK ENGINE
Paintings and photographs of railway scenes have been widely used for jigsaw puzzles. This puzzle features Thomas the Tank Engine, the main character in an ever popular series of children's books written by the Reverend Awdry in the 1940s, and later made into an animated television series and DVD.

SCALED TO SIZE
Accurate working scale models are usually made as a hobby by skilled craftsmen. This live steam coal-fired model, *Lady of Lynn*, is of an express locomotive that ran on the Great Western Railway in Britain in 1908.

Into the future

NEW KINDS OF TRAINS and track are being developed, using new materials and more environmentally friendly power sources. In cities, trains are recognised as the main way to achieve a desired shift away from an over-dependence on the car, to cut both traffic congestion and fuel emissions. This has led to many new electric rapid transit systems being built. New and existing railways provide swift, comfortable cross-country transport and are also helping in the fight against carbon emissions and global warming. Fast electric trains are now standard in most of the developed world with countries such as China and India rapidly catching up. In some countries tilting high-speed trains running on conventional lines provide higher speeds and a more comfortable ride for passengers while avoiding the extra cost of building new lines. Rail freight services are booming again, with new lines being built in many parts of the world for goods. This benefits the environment and has halted the loss of this traffic to the road.

Shanghai Maglev at the Shanghai Pudong International Airport in China

MAGNETIC LEVITATION
This Maglev train works by magnetic levitation. Instead of travelling on wheels on a track, the passenger car (which has no wheels) hovers at 15 mm above a track, propelled along by magnets. This system has many advantages – there are no moving parts to wear out, no maintenance is required, and it makes hardly any noise. The Shanghai Maglev can accelerate to 350 kph (220 mph) in 2 minutes and runs at a maximum speed of 431 kph (268 mph).

DRIVERLESS TRAINS
Light rail transit systems, such as the Docklands Light Railway in London (left), provide a convenient and frequent service in congested city centres. The trains are powered by electricity, which is collected from a shielded third rail along the track. They are driverless, and are operated automatically by computer from a central control room.

The Docklands Light Railway is elevated above street level

Freight trains carry anything from cars, to fuel, or sheep

TRIED AND FAILED
The development of the gas turbine engine soon attracted the interest of railway engineers. The first gas turbine locomotive was built for Swiss Railways in 1941. This picture shows a Canadian National Railway gas turbine-powered train. Like many trains of its kind, it proved to be unreliable, and was withdrawn from service in the mid-1980s.

TAKING THE BEND
Tilting trains developed by the Italian Railways have recently been designed to run on high-speed services on upgraded traditional lines. When a curve is detected by the sensor controls, the train is tilted by a hydraulic mechanism to ensure passenger comfort as it goes through the curve. These electric trains have a maximum speed of 250 kph (155.35 mph). These trains operate on several services in Italy.

SUPER TRAIN
When the Channel Tunnel opened in 1994 trains ran from Waterloo. In 2007 a new terminus opened at London St Pancras International. Eurostar electric train services currently run from London to Paris in two hours fifteen minutes and in under two hours from London to Brussels. Because of the different electrical systems used by the railways concerned, the power cars are equipped to run from three different voltages. There are plans to extend the services.

Eurostar passenger train at St Pancras International

The E200 made its first journey in July 2007

It carries a bank of lithium-ion batteries that recharge every time the brakes are applied

GREEN TRAINS
This E200 train running in Japan includes a unit with a flat screen in the passenger compartment showing how much energy is being used as the train moves. The train is designed to be environmentally friendly, using hybrid power – a motor and batteries with regenerative braking (the batteries recharge every time the train brakes). This cuts noise and emissions by up to 60 per cent. The motor can be powered with hydrogen, biofuel (made from crops) or conventional fossil fuels.

Two freight containers sit on top of each other

DOUBLE DECKER
This double-stack container train is carrying freight on the Cajon Pass in California, on the BNSF Railway. Double-stack container trains carry much more freight than conventional trains, giving a saving in fuel costs per unit, as well as avoiding the major costs of adding tracks to rail routes. The railway is a key part of the world distribution network for goods.

Great train journeys

MORE THAN 1.3 MILLION KM (800,000 miles) of track cross the Earth's landscape, and each year passengers travel over 2,200 billion km (1,367 billion miles) on the world's trains. You can take in spectacular scenery on long-distance trains such as The Canadian, enjoy high-speed thrills on the bullet trains of Japan, or travel in luxury aboard Europe's Orient Express and Africa's Blue Train. For more extreme tastes, try the world's steepest rail climb up the Devil's Nose Mountain in Ecuador, or ride in the only passenger carriage on Mauritania's iron-ore desert train — the world's biggest scheduled train, up to 2.5 km (1½ miles) long.

● THE CANADIAN (CANADA)
As it journeys through the splendid wilderness of the Rockies, the great plains of the prairies, and the scenic lakelands of Ontario, the Canadian hauls its passenger cars 4,466 km (2,775 miles) from Vancouver on the Pacific coast in the west to Toronto in the east.

● CALIFORNIA ZEPHYR (USA)
Running from San Francisco to Chicago, the California Zephyr's 3,924-km (2,438-mile) journey follows the route of the first US transcontinental railroad. It offers dramatic views of the Sierra Nevada Mountains and the upper Colorado River Valley.

Oslo to Bergen (Norway)

NORTH AMERICA

The Canadian

Coast Starlight: Los Angeles to Seattle (USA)

California Zephyr

Road to the Isles: Fort William to Mallaig (Scotland)

Durango and Silverton Railway (USA)

Orient Express: London to Istanbul (trans-Europe)

Havana to Santiago (Cuba)

Glacier Express

Copper Canyon Railway

El Transcantábrico: Santiago de Compostela to Léon (Spain)

Panama Canal Railway: Colón to Panama City (Panama)

Iron-ore desert train: Nouadhibou to Choum (Mauritania)

The Devil's Nose: Riobamba to Sibambe (Ecuador)

Dakar to Bamako (Senegal/Mali)

SOUTH AMERICA

Lima to Huancayo (Peru)

Cusco to Machu Picchu

Belo Horizonte to Vitoria (Brazil)

Oruro to Tupiza (Bolivia)

Curitiba to Paranaguá (Brazil)

● COPPER CANYON RAILWAY (MEXICO)
This 650-km (390-mile) route from Los Mochis, near the Pacific coast, runs through the peaks of the Sierra Madre and across the high central plains to Chihuahua. It takes in some of Mexico's most rugged, breathtaking terrain, including the spectacular Copper Canyon.

● CUSCO TO MACHU PICCHU (PERU)
This spectacular journey to the ancient Inca ruins at Machu Picchu travels 112 km (70 miles) through the Sacred Valley and the foothills of the Andes. Before reaching Machu Picchu, the train travels along the Urubamba River, with awe-inspiring views of the dramatic canyon.

● GLACIER EXPRESS (SWITZERLAND)
Reputed to be the world's slowest express, this train travels 291 km (180 miles) from Zermatt to St Moritz, negotiating 291 bridges and 91 tunnels on the way. It runs on narrow-gauge track and uses rack-rails to climb the steepest slopes along the route.

● TRANS-SIBERIAN RAILWAY (RUSSIA)
Travelling through seven time zones and trundling some 9,288 km (5,771 miles) across Russia, this is the longest rail journey in the world. This epic voyage runs from Moscow in the west via Siberia to Vladivostok in the east beside the Sea of Japan.

● QINGZANG RAILWAY (CHINA)
This 1,956-km (1,215-mile) route from Lhasa, Tibet, to Xining, Qinghai Province, includes the world's highest section of track through the Tanggula Pass at 5,072 m (16,640 ft). To make travel at high altitude easier, the carriages have an oxygen supply for each passenger.

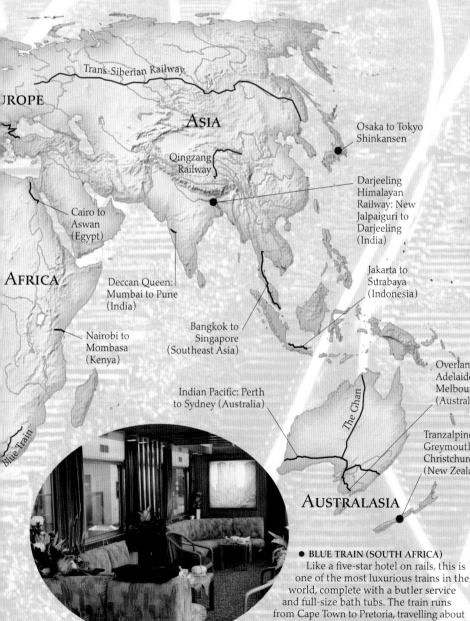

Trans-Siberian Railway

EUROPE

ASIA

Qingzang Railway

Osaka to Tokyo Shinkansen

Darjeeling Himalayan Railway: New Jalpaiguri to Darjeeling (India)

Cairo to Aswan (Egypt)

AFRICA

Deccan Queen: Mumbai to Pune (India)

Jakarta to Surabaya (Indonesia)

Nairobi to Mombasa (Kenya)

Bangkok to Singapore (Southeast Asia)

Indian Pacific: Perth to Sydney (Australia)

Overlander: Adelaide to Melbourne (Australia)

The Ghan

Tranzalpine: Greymouth to Christchurch (New Zealand)

Blue Train

AUSTRALASIA

● OSAKA TO TOKYO SHINKANSEN (JAPAN)
The Osaka–Tokyo Shinkansen was the world's first high-speed train servce. Today, the new, ultra-modern Nozomi bullet trains devour the 525-km (325-mile) route, which passes Mount Fuji, in just two-and-a-half hours, reaching speeds of around 300 kmh (185 mph).

● BLUE TRAIN (SOUTH AFRICA)
Like a five-star hotel on rails, this is one of the most luxurious trains in the world, complete with a butler service and full-size bath tubs. The train runs from Cape Town to Pretoria, travelling about 1,600 km (994 miles) through vineyards, mountains, and the semi-desert of the Karoo.

● THE GHAN (AUSTRALIA)
Running from Darwin south to Adelaide through Australia's dramatic "Red Centre", The Ghan takes 48 hours to travel 2,979 km (1,850 miles) across the continent. The name Ghan refers to the Afghan camel trains that once trekked the same route before the advent of the railways.

Train timeline

AROUND 200 YEARS AGO, railways began to revolutionize our world, opening up new opportunities for travel and trade. At first viewed with suspicion, trains were soon embraced as the technological wonder of the age. This new means of transport could carry people and goods faster and further than ever before. Today, with the world's roads increasingly choked by traffic, railways are making a comeback. This timeline lists some important "firsts" in the history of trains and railways.

1604
A track-way carrying horse-drawn coal wagons on wooden rails is built near Nottingham, UK.

1767
The world's first iron rails for coal wagons are made at Coalbrookedale Iron Works, in Shropshire, UK.

1769
In Paris, France, Nicolas Cugnot builds and demonstrates a steam-powered road carriage – the first ever self-propelled vehicle.

1804
English engineer Richard Trevithick builds the world's first steam locomotive.

1812
The coal-carrying Middleton Railway in Leeds, UK, is the first commercial railway to successfully use steam locomotives.

1825
The Stockton and Darlington Railway in County Durham, UK, is the first public steam railway.

1828
The USA's Delaware & Hudson Railroad is the first operational railway in North America.

1829
George and Robert Stephenson's *Rocket* wins the Rainhill Trials near Liverpool, UK, establishing steam traction as the future of railways.

1830
The UK's Liverpool & Manchester Railway runs the first scheduled steam passenger services.

1830
The *Best Friend of Charleston* is the first all-American-built locomotive.

1837
The first practical electric telegraph instruments are demonstrated in the UK and USA. Telegraphs will be widely used for railway communications.

1841
In the UK, Isambard Kingdom Brunel opens the Great Western Railway from London to Bristol.

1843
The steamship *Great Britain* combines with the express trains of the Great Western Railway to link London, UK, with New York City, USA.

1853
The first railway in India begins operating.

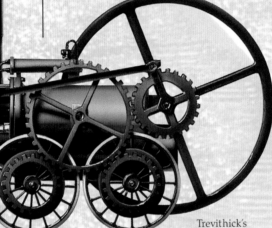

Trevithick's locomotive, 1804

1854
Australia's first railway links Port Melbourne with Melbourne, New South Wales.

1856
In southeastern USA, a railway bridge is built over the Mississippi River for the first time.

1863
The world's first underground railway opens in London, UK. It is steam-powered.

1860
The *Flying Scotsman* begins running between London and Edinburgh, UK.

1863
The first railway is built in New Zealand.

1869
The Transcontinental Railroad spans North America from east to west.

1869
In the USA, George Westinghouse demonstrates his air braking system.

The Golden Spike Ceremony at the opening of the US Transcontinental Railroad, 1869

1871
New York City's Grand Central Station opens. It is the world's largest railway station.

1881
The world's first public electric railway opens in Germany at Lichterfelde, near Berlin.

1885
The Canadian Pacific Railroad begins operating.

1890
An electric underground railway opens in London – it is the first of its kind in the world.

1893
The world's first electric overhead railway opens in Liverpool, UK.

1895
The Baltimore & Ohio Railroad, USA, is the first main line railway to be electrified in the world.

1903
In Germany, an AEG single electric railcar reaches 210 kph (130 mph).

1904
The Trans-Siberian Railway opens from Moscow to Vladivostok, Russia.

1904
Opening of the New York City Subway.

1913
The world's first regular diesel-train service begins in Sweden.

1928
The UK's *Flying Scotsman* service runs non-stop between London and Edinburgh, covering the 632-km (393-mile) route in 8 hours 3 minutes.

1932
Germany's diesel-powered "Flying Hamburger", the first purpose-built high-speed train, begins running between Hamburg and Berlin.

1932
The LMS railway's new shunting locomotives are the first diesels on the UK rail network.

1933
The UK's Southern Railway electrifies the London to Brighton main line.

1934
Streamlined diesel trains begin running between Los Angeles and New York City. The 5,225-km (3,248-mile) journey takes 57 hours.

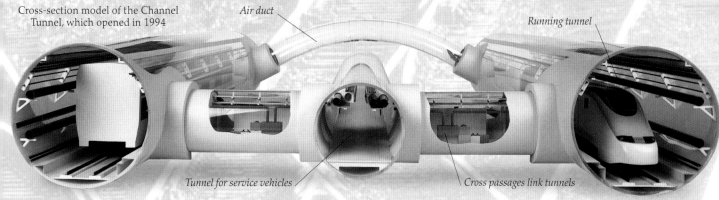

Cross-section model of the Channel Tunnel, which opened in 1994

Air duct

Running tunnel

Tunnel for service vehicles

Cross passages link tunnels

1934
The French railway ETAT introduces a 159-kph (99-mph), lightweight, streamlined petrol railcar designed by Italian car manufacturer Bugatti.

1935
The *Hiawatha* connecting Chicago with Minneapolis/St Paul, USA, is the fastest scheduled steam service in the world.

1935
A world speed record for non-streamlined steam locomotives of 173 kph (108 mph) is set by the UK's LNER A3 locomotive *Papyrus*.

1935
The Moscow subway opens its first line.

Moscow subway

1938
In the UK, the locomotive *Mallard* sets a world record for steam traction of 203 kph (126 mph).

1941
The USA's Union Pacific Railroad unveils its new locomotive, the 4-8-8-4 Big Boy. It is the largest steam locomotive ever built.

1945
The New York Central Railroad reduces the journey time for the 1,493-km (928-mile) New York–Chicago trip to 16 hours.

1949
Canada announces the abolition of steam trains.

1952
"Piggyback" trains that can transport articulated road lorries enter service in North America.

1960
Container trains begin operating in the USA.

1960
The Norfolk & Western Railroad becomes the last class-one US railroad to drop steam traction.

1964
Japan opens the world's first purpose-built high-speed passenger railway – the bullet train. The line speed is 210 kph (130 mph).

1968
Steam power ends on the UK rail network.

1969
Australia opens the east–west transcontinental rail route from Sydney to Perth.

1970
In America, Penn Central Railway goes bankrupt. It is the largest corporate failure in US history.

1971
The US government forms AMTRAK to operate all passenger rail services in the USA.

1981
France opens its first TGV high-speed line between Paris and Lyon. It has a top speed of 300 kph (186 mph).

1984
The first double-stack container trains begin operating in the USA.

1984
The world's first maglev train opens at Birmingham International Airport in the UK.

1987
British Rail's High-Speed Train sets a new record for diesel traction of 238 kph (147mph).

1991
Germany opens its first ICE high-speed rail line.

1994
The Channel Tunnel opens, providing an undersea rail link between the UK and France.

2000
In the USA, AMTRAK launches its Acela Express between Boston and Washington, DC.

2001
In Australia, the world's longest ever train measures 7.3 km (4.5 miles). It consists of 682 cars and eight locomotives.

2003
Japan's experimental maglev train sets a new world speed record of 581 kph (361 mph).

2004
China opens the Shanghai maglev line. Trains can reach 350 kph (220 mph) in two minutes.

2006
China opens the world's highest railway, linking Beijing with Lassa in Tibet, via Xining.

2006
The USA's Union Pacific Railroad sets a world record of 172 million tonnes (194 million tons) of coal moved in one year.

2007
High-Speed One opens a 299-kph (186-mph) connection between London and the European high-speed rail network.

2007
A specially designed French V150 TGV sets a new world record for electric traction of 574 kph (356 mph).

2007
Japan unveils its new N700 "green" bullet train, which delivers high-speed rail services with reduced energy use.

2008
Mumbai, the world's largest city and India's commercial heart, has the world's busiest urban rail system, carrying 6.1 million people each day.

Japan's N700 bullet train, 2007

Find out more

BECAUSE TRAINS ARE SO POPULAR, there is a wealth of places to go to discover more about railways. You can ride historic trains on a heritage railway, join a railway society and help operate and restore trains, or visit transport museums to see railway artefacts from past and present. On some redundant lines, the tracks have been removed to turn them into public paths. Your local library is likely to have railway DVDs and books, and you can surf the Web for rail enthusiast groups, events, and special trains.

Goathland Station, North Yorkshire Moors Railway, UK

USEFUL WEBSITES

- Wikipedia has many articles about railways, famous trains, and railway history: http://en.wikipedia.org/wiki/History_of_rail_transport
- Find out how locomotives, maglevs, and other rail technology works at How Stuff Works. Just type in your terms, and search: www.howstuffworks.com/
- The online technology archive of the London Science Museum has loads of information on railway history and technology: www.makingthemodernworld.org.uk
- The UK's National Railway Museum has a superb website with online exhibitions, photo galleries, movie clips, and audio recordings: www.nrm.org.uk/home/home.asp
- The UK Heritage Railways site has links to almost every railway museum, heritage railway, and rail chat group in the world, along with technical details about locomotives, carriages, and signalling systems: http://ukhrail.uel.ac.uk
- Trainweb is an amazing US site for all things train-related, from trips to videos and fans' pictures: www.trainweb.com
- The National Railroad Museum of America tells the story of how rail shaped the USA: www.nationalrrmuseum.org
- The National Railway Historical Society is the main US umbrella group for all rail fans: www.nrhs.com
- Rails Canada is a directory of websites about trains in Canada, including photo galleries, musems, rail history, and model clubs: www.railscanada.com/index2.shtml
- The website of the National Railway Museum in Port Adelaide, Australia, has online photo exhibitions of locomotives, carriages, railcars, and stations: www.natrailmuseum.org.au
- For details of how to travel by rail anywhere in the world, see: http://www.seat61.com/
- This train simulator fan site hosted on MSN is full of discussions, tutorials, and projects: http://groups.msn.com/TrainSimulatorFanSite

MUSEUM VISITS

Transport museums, and even some science museums, usually have sections devoted to trains, and most countries have a dedicated national railway museum. These are all great places to get an overview of the development of trains and railway technology, from the earliest days of steam up to modern times.

HERITAGE RAILWAYS

Around the world there are many heritage railways where you can still ride on steam trains and sometimes even get a lesson in how to drive a steam locomotive. Heritage railways are generally run by a mixture of paid staff and unpaid volunteers, and have supporting groups that welcome new members.

A steam locomotive at the Swiss Museum of Transport, Lucerne, Switzerland

Trains in the movies

HARRY POTTER FILMS (2002 TO PRESENT)
In these films about a young wizard, a steam train called the Hogwarts Express takes Harry and his pals to wizard school. Hogwarts station is really Goathland (see opposite) on the North Yorkshire Moors Railway.

THE GENERAL (1927)
Buster Keaton's classic silent comedy features a railway engineer who pursues a stolen locomotive in the American Civil War, with amazing train stunts by Keaton himself.

THE POLAR EXPRESS (2004)
A magical train pulls up at a boy's house on the night before Christmas and invites him to travel to the North Pole to meet Santa.

THE RAILWAY CHILDREN (1970)
Based on Edith Nesbit's novel this much-loved film tells the story of children growing up beside a railway track in Victorian England.

Harry Potter and the Chamber of Secrets (2002)

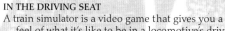

Velorail in Brittany, France

RIDING THE RAILS
In some places, the old trackbeds of disused railways have been given a new lease of life by being turned into paths for walkers and cyclists, enabling you to follow the routes once travelled by locomotives. In France, Sweden, Germany, and some other parts of Europe there are also velorails. Here you can pedal your own "carriage" over sections of preserved track no longer used by trains. Some of these pedal-powered railcycles are refurbished models that were used once by railway workers to check the tracks.

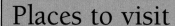

Microsoft® Train Simulator computer game

IN THE DRIVING SEAT
A train simulator is a video game that gives you a feel of what it's like to be in a locomotive's driving seat. This typically involves using the controls in a realistic "virtual" cab to drive the train on a computerized representation of an actual route. More complex versions let you manage freight yards, operate signals, and design your own routes, complete with stations, signals, and scenery. Some simulators can be downloaded free from the Internet. Others can be purchased for use on home PCs.

Places to visit

BALTIMORE & OHIO RAILROAD MUSEUM, BALTIMORE, MARYLAND, USA
The most comprehensive US collection, based at a historic 16-hectare (40-acre) site.

NATIONAL RAILROAD MUSEUM, GREEN BAY, WISCONSIN, USA
Over 70 locomotives and rail cars, including "Big Boy" – the largest locomotive ever.

NATIONAL RAILWAY MUSEUM, YORK, UK
A superb museum, with the world's largest collection of trains and railway artefacts.

NORTH YORKSHIRE MOORS RAILWAY, UK
The UK's most popular heritage steam railway runs through beautiful moorland scenery from Pickering to Grosmont.

SCIENCE MUSEUM, LONDON, UK
Lots of exhibits on railways, including Stephenson's original *Rocket* locomotive.

STATE RAILROAD MUSEUM, SACRAMENTO, CALIFORNIA, USA
This tells the story of California's railroads and their impact on the "golden state".

STEAM, SWINDON, UK
Discover the history of the Great Western Railway and its locomotive works.

SNAPPING AND SPOTTING
Famous and historic locomotives often take to the tracks on special occasions, providing rail enthusiasts with a great opportunity to photograph or ride on their favourite engines. "Train spotting", or collecting the numbers of locomotives still in service, is a more specialized hobby followed by some rail fans.

Glossary

AIR BRAKE A brake that relies on controlling air pressure to apply and release the brake.

ARTICULATED LOCOMOTIVE A long steam locomotive with one or more sets of driving wheels that can move independently from the main body of the locomotive, making it easier to travel round tight bends in the track.

BELL CODE A language for describing trains used by signallers to despatch and receive trains.

BELL TAPPER A device used to tap out bell signals between signallers.

BLOCK A section of railway controlled by a specific signalman or signal tower.

BOGIE A wheeled chassis or framework that is attached to a locomotive or railway carriage by a swivel mounting.

BUCKEYE A form of coupling on a rail vehicle that enables two or more rail vehicles to be joined together to form a train.

BUFFER A shock absorber between rail vehicles.

BULLHEAD RAIL A type of rail developed in the UK, in which the top half of the rail mirrors the bottom half. This design was intended to make rails last longer. Once the running side was worn out, the rail could be turned over and reused.

BULK LOAD A term used to describe a large quantity of freight, such as coal, stone, or grain, that is moved in a single train load.

BRAKE VAN A rail vehicle that provides braking power for goods trains and accommodation for the train guard.

CAB The part of a locomotive or power car from which the driver controls a train.

CARRIAGE A passenger vehicle on a train, also called a car (especially in North America).

CAST IRON A form of iron that can be cast, or moulded, into almost any shape when molten. Cast iron was used to make rails and bridges in the early days of railways. It was later replaced by wrought iron, which is stronger.

CHIMNEY On a steam locomotive, this is the outlet through which all the gases from the fire escape into the air.

COMMUTERS Passengers who use trains to make regular journeys every working day.

CONTAINER A metal freight box that can be packed with goods, sealed, and then transported by specially adapted ships, trains, and trucks.

COUPLING The method of connecting rail vehicles together.

COW CATCHER A metal grill attached to the front of many early US and Indian locomotives, designed to push stray cattle aside from a moving train.

CRANK Part of a steam locomotive that transmits power from the piston to the driving wheels.

CREW A term that usually refers to a steam locomotive's driver or engineer and fireman.

CUTTING A large ditch cut through the landscape to provide a more level route for a railway.

CYLINDER A chamber in an engine in which steam expands or fuel ignites to push pistons back and forth, and so generate power.

DIESEL LOCOMOTIVE A railway locomotive powered by a diesel engine.

DIESEL ELECTRIC LOCOMOTIVE A locomotive with a diesel engine that produces power for electric traction motors, which drive the wheels.

DINING CAR A carriage fitted out for serving food to railway passengers.

DRIVING WHEEL A wheel that propels a locomotive along a track. On a steam locomotive, the driving wheels are powered by the pistons. On diesel and electric locomotives, electric traction motors supply power to the driving wheels.

ELECTRIC TELEGRAPH A communication system developed in the 1830s that used electrical impulses travelling through wires to send messages, including messages in Morse code. It became the standard instrument of railway communication worldwide.

ELECTRIC TRAIN A train that uses electricity drawn from an external source – such as an overhead power line, third rail, or on-board batteries – to power traction motors on the train.

ELEVATED RAILWAY A railway built on raised platforms through city streets. Examples are the former Liverpool Overhead Railway in the UK and part of the New York Subway, USA.

EMBANKMENT An earthen structure designed to raise a railway above the natural ground level.

Diesel locomotive

Cast-iron emblem on a London railway bridge

EXHAUST PIPE The pipe that allows waste gases from a diesel engine to escape.

FIRE BOX A metal box in the heart of a steam locomotive, in which the fire is kept.

FIRE TUBE The fire tube conveys heat from a steam locomotive's fire to the water of its boiler. This boils the water and makes steam.

FISH-BELLY RAIL A type of early cast-iron rail. With its curved, deeper underside it was designed to be stronger than other rails available at the time.

FLANGED WHEEL A railway wheel with a metal lip called a flange on the inside edge.

FLAT-BOTTOMED RAIL The standard rail of today, which takes the form of a T-shape with a wide, flat base.

FREIGHT A term used to describe trains transporting finished goods and raw materials. It can also refer to the load itself.

FUNICULAR RAILWAY Used on tram, cliff, and industrial lines, funicular railways use cables or chains to pull vehicles up and down slopes.

GAUGE The measurement between the rails of a track. The world's most prevalent gauge is 1,435 mm (4 ft 8½ in), and is known as standard gauge. However, many larger and smaller gauges are also used on the world's rail systems.

GAUGE GLASSES A device on a steam locomotive that shows the driver the level of water in the boiler. If the boiler were to run dry, the locomotive would explode.

GUARD The person who is responsible for the operation of a passenger train. In the past, the guard looked after parcels and other freight in a guard's van.

HEADBOARD A notice on the front of a train that gives the train's name, route, or destination.

Funicular railway in Pau, France

INTERMODAL A term used to describe a freight system that changes between different modes of transport, such as from a train to a lorry to a ship. This is what happens with containers.

LEVEL CROSSING A place where a road crosses a railway track on flat ground.

LOCOMOTIVE A self-propelled railway vehicle that can haul a train. There are steam, diesel, and electric locomotives.

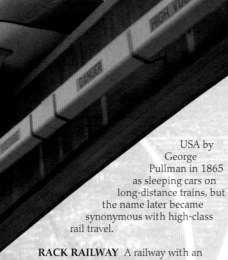

Monorail at Walt Disney World, Florida, USA

MAGLEV TRAIN A train that works by being suspended and propelled over special tracks by electromagnetic force. Maglevs produce virtually no friction, and are very quiet in operation at high speed.

MARSHALLING YARD A place where freight trains are assembled, or where freight wagons for different destinations get moved to the right train.

MONORAIL A train that runs on a single rail.

NAVVY From the word "navigators", hired labourers who built the canals and who went on to build the railway network.

OFF A signal is "off" when it is indicating that a train can proceed.

PANTOGRAPH A device on top of an electric train that collects electric current from the overhead power line.

"PIGGY BACK" A train that can transport whole articulated lorries. This simplifies the transfer of freight between road and rail.

PISTON Part of a steam locomotive that drives the wheels. It consists of a rod inside a cylinder that is pushed in and out by steam. Other rods harness this motion and turn the wheels.

PLATE RAIL L-shaped iron rails used on plateways to guide wagons with plain wheels. (Railway vehicles today have flanged wheels.)

PLATEWAY An early railway that used plate rail, often built as a feeder line to a canal or river.

POINTS Special pieces of track that allow a train to switch from one set of tracks to another.

PULLMAN CAR A luxury railway carriage for passengers who are willing and able to pay a higher fare. Pullmans were introduced in the USA by George Pullman in 1865 as sleeping cars on long-distance trains, but the name later became synonymous with high-class rail travel.

RACK RAILWAY A railway with an additional toothed rack-rail. The train or locomotive is fitted with a cog that links with the teeth on the rack-rail, enabling it to climb slopes that would be impossible for a normal train.

RAILCAR A self-propelled passenger vehicle, usually with the engine located under the floor.

RAILWAY TIME Before railway timetables, different places in the same country often had

Rack railway in Snowdonia, Wales

their own local time. In the 1840s, railways began to introduce a standardized "railway time" to avoid the confusion caused by local time differences.

SHUNTER A small locomotive for moving trucks or wagons around in a marshalling yard.

SIGNAL A fixed unit with an arm or a light that indicates whether a train should stop, go, or slow down. A signal is also what starts a train, whether it is by a whistle, hand gesture, or bell code.

SIGNAL BOX/SIGNAL TOWER A building in which the movement of trains is controlled by use of signals and coded messages sent from one signal box or tower to another.

SLEEPER The cross-piece supporting the rails of a track, made out of wood, concrete, or steel. Early railways often used stone sleeper blocks.

SLEEPING CAR A carriage with beds where passengers can sleep while travelling. Sleeping cars were first used in America in the 1830s.

STEAM LOCOMOTIVE A locomotive that generates steam by boiling water. The steam is then fed to cylinders that drive the wheels.

SUPERHEATER A device fitted into a steam locomotive's boiler that dries out the steam to give a locomotive more power.

TAIL-LIGHT The lamp at the rear of a train. In the UK, a train is not complete without an illuminated rear warning light.

TANK ENGINE A steam engine that carries the water and coal it uses on the locomotive itself, rather than towing it behind in a tender.

TENDER The truck or wagon behind a steam locomotive that holds the locomotive's fuel (generally coal) and water.

TILTING TRAIN A train that can lean into bends (like a motorcyclist does), enabling it to travel faster along a route with a lot of curves.

TOOTHED RAIL An additional rail often used on mountain railways to enable a train to climb a steeper hill than would be possible for a normal train (*see* Rack railway).

TRAILING WHEEL A wheel located behind the driving wheels of a steam locomotive that provides support but which is unpowered.

TRAIN A complete assembly of power unit and wagons or carriages running on rails, whether carrying freight or passengers. If it is just the power unit, then it is a locomotive.

TRAIN FERRIES Ferries designed to take rail vehicles by having a deck with tracks.

TRUCK A small rail wagon.

VACUUM BRAKE A type of brake that is held off by a partial vacuum, and applied when air is let into the system. Vacuum brakes were used in the UK during the steam era, because unlike air brakes they did not require a separate pump.

WAGON A rail vehicle for carrying freight.

Loading rail trucks in Ghana, Africa

WROUGHT IRON A form of iron that is worked by being forged or hammered, and which was used before the invention of steel.

Index

AB

Adelaide, Queen, 44
"Agenoria" locomotive, 18
American railroad, 18-19
Atchison, Topeka & Santa Fe railway, 30
Atlantic Coast Express, 55
Awdry, Reverend, 61
Baltimore and Ohio Railroad, 18, 38
Bennie, George, 59
"Best Friend of Charleston" locomotive, 12
Beyer-Garratt locomotives, 17, 53
"Blue Train", 42
bogies, 15, 19, 22, 23
boiler, 14, 15, 17, 18, 22, 23
brakes, 8, 9, 15, 26, 27, 34, 35, 60
bridges, 6, 18, 20-21, 22, 23, 54, 61
British Rail, 40, 41, 52, 54
Brunel, Isambard Kingdom, 21
Burlington Route, USA, 41

C

Canadian National Railway, 63
carriages, 6, 7, 10, 16, 19, 20, 28-29, 39, 41, 42, 44, 45, 48
"Catch-me-who-can" train, 10
Central Pacific Railroad, 18
Channel Tunnel, 21, 63
chimney, 15, 18, 23, 54, 57
Chinese National Railway, 17
Christie, Agatha, 31
clockwork trains, 60, 61
coal, 7, 8, 9, 14, 15, 19, 26, 44, 53, 61
coal-wagons, 9, 10, 11, 27

compartments, 28, 29, 31, 44, 45
cowcatchers, 13, 19
Cugnot, Nicholas, 10

DE

"Deltic" locomotives, 40, 41
Der Adler locomotive, 16
"De Witt Clinton", 19
diesel-electric trains, 7, 12, 26, 41
Diesel, Dr. Rudolph, 40
diesel power, 40-41, 52, 53, 59
diesel trains, 6, 7, 26, 38, 40
dining cars, 7, 30, 43, 51
Docklands Light Railway, 62
Dominion Atlantic Railway, 55
drivers, 11, 15, 19, 33, 34, 35, 41, 49, 50, 56
driving wheels, 11, 14, 15, 19
East Indian Railways, 16
Edward VII, King, 45
electric power, 52, 53, 59
electric trains, 6, 7, 12, 18, 38-39, 40, 47, 56, 58, 62, 63
"Empire State Express", 47
engines, 8, 10, 26, 40, 41, 46
Evans, Oliver, 11
"Evening Star", locomotive, 52
express trains, 13, 39, 41, 51, 52, 54, 56

FG

fireman, 15, 50
first-class travel, 6, 28, 29, 30, 41
Firth of Forth bridge, 23
flanged rails, 8, 10, 25
flanged wheels, 7, 8, 9, 18, 24, 25
"Flying Scotsman", 13
freight, 7, 9, 25, 39, 41, 48, 49, 58
freight trains, 6, 12, 26-27, 50, 52, 56, 60, 61, 62
Gare de Lyon, Paris, 49

gauge, 24, 25, 52
"Gladstone" locomotive, 44
gradients, 20, 22, 23, 39, 47
Grand Central Station, 48
Great Western Railway, 50, 55, 61
Gresley, Sir Nigel, 47
guards, 26, 29, 34, 50, 51, 56

HIJK

headboards, 54-55, 57
headlamps, 13, 16, 19, 44
Hedley, William, 11
"Hiawatha" service, 46
high-speed trains, 22, 34, 37, 38, 39, 41, 47, 62, 63
ICE train, 47
"Indian Pacific" train, 42
Inter-Capitals Supertrains, 63
inter-city trains, 41, 47
International Railway Station, Birmingham, 63
"Irish Mail" train, 37
Italian Railways, 63
"John Bull" locomotive, 19
junctions, 32, 35, 50
Kitson-Meyer locomotive, 22

L

"Lady of Lynn" locom..
"Le Mistral" train, 38
Liverpool and Manchester Railway, 6, 12, 13
Llanberis Lake Railway, 52
locomotives, 36, 44, 60, articulated, 17, diesel, 6, 7, 38, diesel-electric, 7, 12, 26, electric, 6, 12, 38, 39, 40, 56, gas turbine, 63, steam, 6, 7, 8, 10, 11, 12-19, 20, 24, 26, 39, 46, 47, 51, 52-53, 54, 57, 61, tank, 22, 53, 57
London, Chatham and Dover Railway, 49
London North Eastern

Railway, 46
long-distance railways, 42-43, 51

MNO

Maglev train, 62
mail train, 8, 36-37
"Mallard" locomotive, 41, 46, 47
Mary, Queen, 45
Metro, 56, 57
Metropolitan Railway, 57
model trains, 60-61
monorails, 58-59
Montmartre Funicular, Paris, 58
Mount Washington Railway, 23
mountain railways, 22, 23
nameplates, 54-55
National Motor Museum, Beaulieu, 58
National Railway Museum, 52
"navvies", 6, 20
New York Central Railroad, 47
Newcomen, Thomas, 10
Norris, William
North Eastern Railway, 39
"Novelty" locomotive, 5, 12
"Orient Express", 31, 43, 46

P

pantograph, 38, 39
Paris *Metro*, 57
passenger service, 7, 52, 62
passenger trains, 12, 13, 21, 28-29, 37, 39, 47, 50
piston, 10, 14, 15, 40
points, 24, 32, 33, 34, 61
pollution, 7, 18, 58, 62
porters, 48, 50
"Puffing Billy" locomotive, 11
Pullman Company, 30, 31
Pullman, George, 30

QR

railroads, 13, 18-19, 27
rails, 7, 8, 11, 18, 20, 24-25, 48, 58, 59, 63, flanged, 10, 25, iron, 9, 24, steel, 24, 25
railway, 6, 7, 10, 12, 13, 16, 19, 20, 23, 29, 32, 37, 42, companies, 54, earliest, 8-9, elevated, 58, 59, funicular, 58, hotels, 30, lines, 24-25, mountain, 22, network, 26, overhead, 58-59, police, 34, straddle, 58-59, suspended, 58-59, underground, 56-57, 58
rapid transport system 38, 56, 62, 63
restaurant cars, 28, 30, 38, 42
"Rocket" locomotive, 7, 13
Royal Albert Bridge, Plymouth, 21
Royal Mail, 37

S

self-propelled vehicles, 6, 10, 11
Shinkansen railway, 47
shunting, 26, 35, 41, 50
signalmen, 32-33, 34, 50, 56
signals, 15, 32-35, 51, 61
signal boxes, 7, 20, 25, 30,
Snowdon Mountain Railway, 23
South Eastern Railway, 52
stations, 21, 24, 30, 33, 34, 37, 42, 44, 46, 48-49, 50, 54, 56, 57, 61
steam, 10-11, 38, 52, 53, 56, 60, engines, 8, 10, 40, 41, 46, locomotives, 12-19, 20, 24, 26, 39, 47, 51, 52-53, 54, 57, 61, trains, 6, 9, 17, 19, 23, 29, 50
Stephenson, George, 12
Stephenson, Robert, 7, 12, 13, 19
Stockton and Darlington Railway, 12
"Stourbridge Lion"

locomotive, 18
"Super Chief" service, 43
Swiss Railways, 63
Sydney Harbour Bridge, 22

T

TEE, 41
tender, 7, 14, 15, 17, 18
TGV, 39, 47, 54
"The Caledonian", 55
"The Russia" train, 42
"Thomas the Tank Engine", 61
tickets, 28, 48, 49
tilting trains, 37, 39, 62, 63
"Tom Thumb" locomotive, 18
toothed rack, 11, 23
toy trains, 60-61
train ferries, 23, 43
Trans-Siberian Express, 42
Travelling Post Office, 36-37
Trevithick, Richard, 10
tube trains, 56-57
tunnels, 6, 20-21, 38, 39, 54, 56, 57, 61

UVWXYZ

underground railways, 7, 38, 56, 57, 58
Union Pacific Railroad, 18, 61
Victoria, Queen, 44, 45
von Siemens, Werner, 38
Wagons-Lits Company, 43
Waterloo Station, London, 49
Watt, James, 10
Western Australian Government railways, 55
whistle, 19, 49, 51, 60
"Winston Churchill", 54
"Zephyr" train, 41
Zimbabwe Railways, 53

Acknowledgements

Dorling Kindersley would like to thank:
Staff at the National Railway Museum, York, especially David Wright and Richard Gibbon; John Liffen at the Science Museum; Justin Scobie for photographic assistance; The London Transport Museum; the signal box staff of Three Bridges (British Rail) Station, West Sussex; The Bluebell Railway; Gatwick Airport; Claire Gillard for initial research; Helena Spiteri and Gin von Noorden for editorial assistance; Earl Neish for design assistance; Jane Parker for the index.

For this edition, the publisher would also like to thank: Robert Gwynne and Russell Hollowood at the National Rail Museum, York, for assisting with the updates; Lisa Stock for editorial assistance; David Ekholm-JAlbum, Sunita Gahir, Susan Reuben, Susan St Louis, Lisa Stock, and Bulent Yusuf for the clipart; Sue Nicholson and Edward Kinsey for the wallchart; Stewart Wild and Monica Byles for proofreading.

Picture credits
The publisher would like to thank the following for their kind permission to reproduce their photographs:

(Key: a-above; b-below/bottom; c-centre; f-far; l-left; r-right; t-top)
Advertising Archives: 26bc, 61tl (detail), 61tr (detail). **Alamy Images:** Steve Crise / Transtock Inc. 62b; Michael Grant 70clb;

JTB Photo Communications, Inc. 65bl, 65tl; James Lovell 68tr; Iain Masterton 67br; Sami Sarkis France 69tl; Nick Suydam 64cla. **alimdi.net:** Photographers Direct 68br. **Aquarius Library:** Warner Bros 69tr. **Australian Overseas Information Service, London:** 42cl. **Barlow Reid:** 7acr, 39cr, 41cr. **Bettmann Archive / Hulton Picture Library:** 19t, 20c. **Bridgeman Art Library / Science Museum, London:** 11btc; National Railway Museum, York:11tr; Private Collections: 13btc; Guildhall Art Gallery, Corporation of London: 45cl; Guildhall Library, Corporation of London: 56cl. **Britt Allcroft (Thomas Ltd), 1989:** 61cl. **Jean-Loup Charmet:** 10bcr, 30bl, 39tr, 44cl, 56cr. **J.A. Coiley:** 54cr, 58br. **G. Cooke, Rail Safaris:** 53cl. **Corbis:** Eleanor Bentall 65br; Ursula Gahwiler / Robert Harding World Imagery 64tr; Colin Garratt, Milepost 92 _71br; Gavin Hellier / Robert Harding World Imagery 67cl; Dave G. Houser 64bc; Lester Lefkowitz 64-71 (background); Bruno Morandi / Robert Harding World Imagery 65tc; Michael Reynolds / EPA 65tr; Phil Schermeister 64bl; Naoaki Watanabe / amanaimages 65cr. **Culver Pictures Inc.:** 11tl, 16btr, 19br, 37tl, 41btr, 47btr. **DeltaRail:** 33tl. **Michael Dent:** 23cl, 52c, 55cr. **DK Images:** Rough Guides 71cb, 71tl. **Docklands Light Railway Ltd / Marysha Alwan:** 62c. **drr.net:** Joern Sackermann 69bc. **e.t. archive:** 6c, 7cl, 9tl, 9tc, 9cl, 12cl, 16bl, 20tr, 26btr (detail), 28tr, 29cr, 33ca, 36tr, 46cl,

49bcl, 51tr. **Eurostar:** 63cra. **Ffotograff:** 42tr. **Getty Images:** Hulton Archive / Andrew Joseph Russell / MPI 66br. **Hulton Picture Company:** 31btl. **Hutchison Picture Library:** 22tl, 53tr. **Japan Railways Group, New York Office:** 63clb. **Antony J. Lambert:** 45c, 60cl. **La vie du rail, Paris:** 38cl, 39tl, 63tl. **Mack Sennet Productions:** 25btr. **Mansell Collection Ltd:** 8tr, 10acr, 23tc. **Mary Evans Picture Library:** 8br, 9cr, 13t, 17btl, 21bcl, 29tl, 35tc, 38c, 40tl, 61bcr. **John Massey Stewart:** 45bcl, 56tr, 59tr. **Microsoft:** Microsoft product screen shot reprinted with permission from Microsoft Corporation. 69c. **Millbrook House Ltd:** 7tr, 23br, 37tr, 51btl, 58cr, 63tr. **National Railway Museum:** 6cl, 7tl, 12tr, 13btr, 21tl, 23tr, 25tr, 25bcr, 26bcl, 30bc, 35cr, 37btc, 43bcr, 49tc, 50cr, 59tl; Terence Cuneo: 33bc. **PA Photos:** DPA Deutsche Press-Agentur / DPA 62tr. **Peter Newark's Picture Library:** 13c, 18tl, 18cr, 19c, 19tr, 24tr, 34tl, 42bl, 43br, 53tl. **Picture Alliance:** DPA 35br **Quadrant Picture Library:** 21c, 27btc, 43btr, 47btl, 47c, 53cr. **Rank Films:** 49bl **Retrograph Archive / Martin Breese:** 36tl. **Robert Harding Picture Library:** 52cl, 58bl, 59cr. **Telegraph Colour Library:** 50tr, 57c. **Weintraub / Ronald Grant:** 31tl. **Zefa Picture Library:** 24tl, 35tl, 41tr, 47t, 48br, 59b

cla (Stephenson's Rocket), clb (diesel locomotive), clb (train tickets), cl (tea set), cl (ticket clippers), cra (wheel), tr (workman's pick); Science Museum, London tl (Trevithick's train); **PA Photos:** DPA Deutsche Press-Agentur / DPA bl (Maglev train); **Photolibrary:** imagebroker cr; **Science & Society Picture Library:** NRM - Pictorial Collection cl (illustration).

All other images © Dorling Kindersley For further information see: **www.dkimages.com**

Wallchart
Corbis: José Fuste Raga / zefa br; **DK Images:** National Railway Museum, York